The GRIEF RECOVERY Handbook

The
GRIEF RECOVERY
Handbook

A Step-by-Step Program
for Moving Beyond Loss

JOHN W. JAMES
& FRANK CHERRY

Co-founders of the Grief Recovery Institute

HARPER & ROW, PUBLISHERS 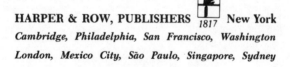 New York
Cambridge, Philadelphia, San Francisco, Washington
London, Mexico City, São Paulo, Singapore, Sydney

FIRST EDITION

Designer: Ruth Bornschlegel

Copyeditor: Ann Adelman

Library of Congress Cataloging-in-Publication Data
James, John W.
    The grief recovery handbook.

    Includes index.
    1. Grief.   2. Loss (Psychology)   I. Cherry, Frank.
II. Title.
BF575.G7J36   1988   152.4   87-46148
ISBN 0-06-015939-1

88   89   90   91   92   HC   10   9   8   7   6   5   4   3   2   1

To our families

and to all of you
who are moving beyond loss

Contents

Introduction

It seems as if we have been doing work with grievers for as long as we can remember. We are the co-founders of the Grief Recovery Institute and the co-authors of this book. Our names are John W. James and Frank Cherry. Although we are both educated in the related fields of education and communications, it is our personal experiences that qualify us to write this book. It is the large number of personal losses each of us experienced that led us to the point of searching for and applying the actions laid out here. As the result of these many losses, we are able to share with you our personal discoveries.

We also draw on our professional experience as grief recovery educators and counselors. The bulk of this work has been in training other caregivers how to talk simply and effectively to the bereaved about their normal and natural reactions to loss, called "grief." We will share with you the results of our work with over a thousand funeral homes, cemeteries, hospitals, and churches throughout the United States and Canada. And we will share with you the common but unique experiences of loss and recovery that we have been privileged to participate in with the thousands of individual grievers we have met in the past ten years.

As our professional programs expanded, it became quite clear to us that there was a need for greater education about grief in every community. To address this need, we devised a program of weekly support group meetings, called Grief Recovery Outreach Programs, that would be sponsored by the professionals we had trained. In a very short time we realized these groups needed a structured plan of action for helping individual participants work through the pain caused by loss. There is nothing more frustrating to a griever than to work very hard on his or her recovery and yet not experience any real change. We also received calls from people who had heard about our work and wanted to join a support group but couldn't because an Outreach Program had not been established in their area.

No matter how hard or long we worked, no matter how many professionals we trained, no matter how many support groups were started, it didn't seem that we were doing enough. The number of people still in pain years after a loss is staggering. We were constantly looking for ways and ideas that would allow us to contact larger numbers of hurting people faster. After much soul searching, planning, and encouragement from professionals, we wrote the first edition of this handbook. Our purpose was, first, to help individuals recover from their grief, and then, ultimately, to change the way each of us responds to those suffering from loss.

We published five thousand copies of the book ourselves to supply the Outreach Programs and the single individuals who had contacted us. We thought that five thousand would last us for a long time—within eight weeks we were out of books. Of course we were pleased to learn that so many people had found the handbook to be of help, but we had also learned that we did not want to remain in the publishing business.

Since that time, this handbook has been enhanced and published for you. We are very grateful that the staff at Harper & Row have bent over backward to help us make this material available to the huge numbers of people who both want and need assistance with ending their pain.

Before we begin, we want to acknowledge and thank all the wonderful people who have researched and written about the topic of grief. We want to acknowledge and thank all of those loving and caring people who have dedicated their lives to helping the bereaved. We want to thank those individuals, organizations, and firms that have helped us to reach the wonderful people we've been honored to work with. Most of all we want to acknowledge, thank, and encourage all those who have been, and all those who will be, involved with the Outreach Programs. You have not only helped us in our work but have already brought aid and comfort to many whom we could never reach personally.

If you have just opened this book, we already feel as if we know you. We want to thank you in advance for all the help you will be to others. We may never meet you personally, we may never see your face, we may never know your name, but we thank you for helping yourself, the Grief Recovery Institute, and all those to whom you will bring a message of hope throughout the rest of your life.

John and Frank

PART ONE

Seeing the Problem

1

Grief Recovery: A Neglected Growth Process

Grieving is the most misunderstood and neglected growth process a person can go through. While we commonly think of education and relationship-building as growth processes, and we've all heard that we should "learn from our mistakes," when we hear the words "grieving" and "growth" in the same sentence, we are likely to be surprised. For many, seeing the title of this book is the first time they have ever seen the terms "grief" and "recovery" used together. Religious and spiritual leaders for centuries have pointed out that we should look at loss as an opportunity for personal spiritual development. Yet in modern life the process of moving through intense emotional pain has become so private and misunderstood that most of us have very little idea of what the process is or how to deal with it.

The Concept of Grief

Simply put, grief is a normal and natural response to loss. The circumstance that comes most readily to mind when we speak of grief is the death of a loved one. Grief is the feeling of reaching out for someone who has always been there, only to find that when we need them one last time, they are no longer there. Yet death is not all we grieve for. Grief is a conflicting mass of human emotion that we experience following any major change in a familiar pattern of behavior.

We grieve for the loss of all relationships that could be held as significant and therefore emotional: moving from one house to another in early childhood can be such an event. Leaving the routine of the home to start school can cause grief for many children. Divorce can cause enormous conflict and confusion. Even marriage can cause feelings of loss for a familiar lifestyle. Dealing with addictions to alcohol, drugs, food, and so on can lead to monumental grief. Retirement, that so many look forward to, can create intense conflicting emotions. Often, these common life experiences are not seen as grieving events.

But we have seen the principles discussed in this book work for those who have experienced the loss of children, spouses, parents, siblings, jobs, farms, lawsuits, drugs, and alcohol. The same solutions have worked for all of these courageous people. We urge you to stay open to what is being offered here.

STAYING OPEN TO GRIEF

We've all heard the statement, "The only things that are certain in life are death and taxes."

Those of you who are reading this book know that one more item must be added to these certainties: loss. We all experience loss many times in our lives. Yet, ironically, despite the inevitability and universality of the experience of loss, we know very little about recovery from it.

What we do know about grievers is that they've always wanted to recover. They seek help from all available sources. Grievers attend support groups; they read pamphlets; they buy books. After having done all these things they're still confronted with the fact that our entire society is ill-equipped to help them bring the grieving experience to a successful conclusion. Over time the pain of unresolved grief is cumulative. Whether the grief was caused by a death or some other type of loss, incomplete recovery can have a lifelong effect on a person's capacity for happiness.

If you ask grievers about all the things they've done, they'll tell you that each action has brought some small amount of relief. They'll also tell you that deep down they know the loss is not yet complete. Small reminders during the day can start the pain over again. Their zest for life has just not come back. It's as if no matter what they do, their lives are still limited and restricted. Having a good day just doesn't mean what it used to. They talk with their doctor, their clergy, their counselors, and with their friends. Yet, for the most part, the grief continues.

Years ago we discovered that there is little or no specific training available in the area of grief recovery skills. There are books and some classes on how to recognize stages of grief, but there is no precise educational technique available on what to say to a grieving person, or how and when to say it. We don't want to paint a totally bleak picture because there are some doctors, nurses, clergy, psychologists, counselors, funeral professionals, and volunteers who have gone to extraordinary lengths to learn. We are friends with many of these professionals through our own seminars and training.

The pioneering work of Dr. Elisabeth Kübler-Ross into the stages of grief experienced by dying people is legendary. Her life's work has led to a more loving, caring, and humane treatment of the dying. Her work is primarily responsible for the development and expansion of the hospice movement and for the more loving concern for families of dying people in many hospitals around the world. Both happily and sadly this progress could not have come at a better time as we struggle to cope with the devastation of AIDS.

Dr. Kübler-Ross identified five stages of grief that accurately define the path to acceptance for a dying patient. In brief, the stages are:

1. Denial

2. Anger

3. Bargaining

4. Depression

5. Acceptance

Many times these stages can also be applied to the bereaved. But in their origin, these stages were observed in the dying patient, not in the grievers left behind. Therefore, our experience has shown us that these stages do not necessarily occur in the same order for the bereaved as they do for the terminally ill, and some stages, such as bargaining, may be passed by the griever entirely. So the path leading to acceptance that a dying person will traverse may not be a sufficient guide for the griever moving toward recovery. If you have found that the available information and support has not satisfied your desire for recovery from loss, it is not because of what's wrong with you—it's because of a lack of information.

If you're reading this book, it means you're open to your grief. It means you're open to beginning a process of recovery that could actually enhance your life rather than limit it. If you're reading this book, it's because of what's right with you, not what's wrong.

THE CONCEPT OF RECOVERY

Now, just what do we mean by "recovery"? Recovery is feeling better. Recovery means claiming your circumstances instead of your circumstances claiming your happiness. Recovery is finding new meaning for living without the fear of future abandonment. Recovery is being able to enjoy fond memories without having them precipitate painful feelings of loss, guilt, regret, or remorse. Recovery is acknowledging that it is perfectly all right to feel bad from time to time and to talk about those feelings no matter how those around you react. Recovery is being able to forgive others when they say or do things that you know are based on their lack of knowledge about grief. Recovery is one day realizing that your ability to talk about the loss you've experienced is in fact helping another person get through his or her loss.

Recently, Frank attended a meeting to establish a new Outreach Program of the Grief Recovery Institute. At the end of the day, the sponsor invited him to her house for dinner. The decor and surroundings reminded him of what his sister's home looked like years before she died; Early American decorations were her favorite and this type of design was quite an avocation for her. The same seemed to be true of the sponsor. Such creativity has always impressed Frank deeply, since he can't even make his desk look attractive. He commented on this to the sponsor.

Later, after returning home, Frank found himself reflecting on what a good time he'd had on his trip. Days afterward, it occurred to him that not once were the reminders of his sister a painful experience; he truly had not had one painful moment as a result of thinking of his sister. He had just had a good time and enjoyed his stay at the sponsor's home. His recovery had given him a wonderful sense of freedom to simply enjoy the moment.

It had taken Frank over five years to get to that point. *But it absolutely need not take five years to achieve a state of freedom, acceptance, and new meaning after the death of a loved one, no matter what the nature of the relationship or the circumstances surrounding the death.* It is precisely these types of experiences and searching that brought us to the writing of this book and having these tools to offer.

Obviously, recovering from a significant emotional loss is not an easy task. It will require your attention, a level of open-mindedness, much willingness, courage, and above all a series of actions and small steps that must be made by you. No one can recover you but you. We can't recover you. This book can't recover you. With the right information and correct action, you can discover the strength within yourself to recover. Getting the proper information to you is what this book is all about. If you have the proper information, then you'll know what the next action is. The next action for you right now is to continue your reading.

How to Use *The Grief Recovery Handbook*

Don't jump ahead in your reading of this handbook, although you may want to. There is a difference between those who resolve their pain and those who don't. The ones who do recover follow a well-defined plan. What we want you to do is follow such a plan so that you can be successful.

The first part of this book is devoted to examining the misinformation you have learned about grief. You'll start to see why it was virtually impossible to recover with the tools you've had to work with. You could try to build a house without a hammer and nails, but it would be impossible for you to succeed. You will soon discover that succeeding in recovery from loss with the tools you've been working with is equally impossible.

The second part of this book will deal with the preparations necessary for recovery. There will be directions to follow with notes of encouragement. In this second part you will discover the essential rules for recovery. It is important that you consider each one of them.

The third part of the book introduces you to the solution. The solution is made up of five stages you must move through in order to recover from a grieving experience. These stages are:

1. Gaining Awareness
2. Accepting Responsibility
3. Identifying Recovery Communications
4. Taking Actions
5. Moving Beyond Loss

This handbook is designed to give you the information necessary to recover from loss. It has much to offer anyone interested in feeling better. If you will simply use it, one word at a time, it will accelerate your recovery tenfold. It also has much to offer anyone interested in helping others feel better as a result of grief.

We know from our own personal and professional experience that never before has there been such a clearly defined plan to follow. Any well-defined plan is analogous to a road map. In order for a road map to be of value, it helps to follow the directions. You might be able to get to Chicago from the south without orienting the map north; then again, you might not get there at all. In order for this book to be successful, you must follow the directions. Throughout the text there will be suggestions, notes, and rules for you to follow. Please don't take any shortcuts with your recovery. Stay on the track. Where recovery from grief is the objective, the consequences that may result from getting lost are too great.

In the next chapter we will discuss how loss of trust is a normal reaction to significant emotional loss. If you're not yet convinced that you're in safe hands, see if you can summon the willingness to keep reading anyway.

Not once will we say:

"We know how you feel."

Not once will we say:

"You should be grateful that you had them for so long."

Not once will we say:

"Now you know they wouldn't have wanted you to feel this way."

And never will we leave you with:

"It just takes time to grieve."

We *will* say that significant emotional loss is an abnormal event in a person's life, and that there is no normal way to react to an abnormal event. We *will* say that we live in a society that doesn't educate us to deal with loss but rather teaches us how to acquire and hold on to things. We *will* say that there are ways to expedite your recovery. The rest of the handbook will show you how.

2

We Are Ill-Prepared to Deal with Loss

Shortly after the loss you experienced, you probably became acutely aware of how ill-prepared you were to deal with the conflicting mass of emotions we call grief.

The same is true for almost everyone in our society. We are far better prepared to deal with minor accidents than we are to deal with the grief caused by death. Simple first aid gets more attention in our world than death and emotional loss. Please don't think we're exaggerating. Stop and consider your own experience. In grade school you took a class on first aid; in high school you took a class on health and safety; the local Red Cross offers classes on first aid in the community. You're probably prepared to take action if an accident occurs in your presence. Nationwide, we have a convenient 911 number to call in case of emergency. At some level we're all prepared to aid an accident victim. How many classes have you taken on how to deal with the grief caused by death or loss? We think it's a little strange that we all know what to do if someone breaks an arm, but no one's prepared to assist grievers, although there are 8 million new ones caused from deaths alone each year.

Each of us has already learned many incorrect things about processing the feelings caused by loss. If we had no knowledge about dealing with grief, it would be better than what we currently know. If the slate of our mind was clean, it would be easier to acquire correct information about what to do.

WE'RE TAUGHT HOW TO ACQUIRE THINGS, NOT HOW TO LOSE THEM

In all our formative learning, the overwhelming emphasis is placed on learning how to acquire both material and nonmaterial things in order to make life a successful and happy event.

In early childhood we try to acquire our parents' praise. Later, we try to acquire toys at Christmas or Hannukah by being good. We try to acquire good grades in school in order to gain approval. We try to look good for our peers so we'll be accepted. This process of learning how to acquire things continues unabated even into our adult lives. Certainly the advertising industry understands this phenomenon when its marketing campaigns focus on finding happiness and contentment through the acquisition of things.

Since almost everything we've learned is about what we can acquire in order to feel complete or whole, the process of losing something feels wrong, unnatural, or broken. Almost everything we've learned about dealing with loss is inappropriate or inadequate for recovering from grief. Now what can we do about it? Many times, before we can solve a problem, it's necessary to break it down into workable components. Everything we've learned has been learned in three steps. First we perceive a need for a skill, then we acquire the components involved, finally we practice the components until we acquire the skill.

The first part of this handbook will assist you in identifying a need to do this work. Later chapters will show you the steps to take in order to deal with loss in a new way. And there will be accounts of our own experiences and those of other grievers in taking these steps toward recovery. But, ultimately, your recovery is up to you. You must supply the need and you must do the practicing. As with most things that work, there is no other way.

WE'RE TAUGHT MYTHS ABOUT DEALING WITH GRIEF

Before we can discuss what recovery is, it's important to look at what it isn't. We must be clear about why we need to find a new way of dealing with loss. We can begin by clarifying our understanding of how we have dealt with loss in the past. We can use John's experiences with loss as an illustration.

John's first memory about learning to deal with loss comes from when he was five years old:

"We had a family dog. This dog adopted me from the moment I arrived home from the hospital. When I was old enough to crawl, I'd pull the dog's tail and she'd let me get away with it. The dog would go everywhere with me. As I grew older, I tried to teach the dog to retrieve. (To this day, I'm not sure who taught whom to retrieve.) The dog always found a way to sleep with me each night. This drove my mother to distraction. But the dog and I were persistent and eventually she gave up.

"Then, one morning, I called to my dog and she wouldn't get up. I remember how cold she felt when I touched her. I remember being afraid. I called to my mother to help me. My mother told me that my dog had died. I'm certain she tried to explain what death was. I'm also certain she didn't know how."

For the next several days after the dog died, John cried a lot and spent a great deal of time in his room. "My parents felt inadequate in knowing what to do to help me," he remembers.

Finally, in total frustration, John's father said:

"Don't feel bad, on Saturday we'll get you a new dog."

Now, that doesn't sound like such a profound sentence. But let's take a closer look. Earlier, we mentioned that we learn by several different methods or processes. One of these is called "influence learning."

A child is born into a family. During the first few years, the child's primary contact is with his or her parents. The child learns from watching and emulating what it sees its parents do. Usually, by eighteen to twenty-four months, the child gains verbal skills. At this point, the child can not only see what its parents are doing but understands what they say. Now John's father had said to him:

"Don't feel bad . . ."

Meaning: Bury your feelings.

". . . On Saturday we'll get you a new dog."

Meaning: Replace the loss.

John was starting to get the picture. He began to form a belief about dealing with loss. He tried to be strong and to follow his father's advice. To a young child who wanted his parents' approval, this was a powerful communication from the most important authority figure in his life. As John explains, "I thought, if this is the way my father deals with death, then this is the way I'm supposed to deal with it."

The real message was that if you lose something, you should replace it as soon as possible. Replacing the loss will make it easier.

Sure enough, on Saturday John's dad took him to the kennel and they got a new dog:

"I still missed my old dog but I didn't tell anyone. I didn't think they'd approve. After a long period of time I actually forgot about my old dog. I also found it hard to love the new dog in the same way I'd loved my old dog, and I didn't know why."

It's possible, in fact likely, that John couldn't love the new dog because he wasn't finished with the old dog.

Several years later someone stole John's bike. As we stated earlier, we grieve for many losses other than death. The loss (or theft) of the bike caused him to be both angry and sad. Once again, his parents were there to tell him:

"Don't feel bad, on Saturday we'll get you a new bike."

They didn't know it, but they were reinforcing the prior messages "Bury your feelings" and "Replace the loss."

When John was fourteen, he fell in love for the first time. It may have been puppy love, but it sure felt like the real thing to him:

"It was wonderful. I was preoccupied with thoughts of her all the time. I had trouble eating and sleeping. The birds sang. I listened to love songs on the radio. I didn't hang out with my friends as much.

"When we broke up I was devastated. This was a major loss for me. For days, I wandered around like a wounded duck. Finally, my mother couldn't take it any more."

What his mother said was:

"Don't feel bad, there are plenty of fish in the sea."

By this point, John had gotten some pretty clear idea about what to do when you lose something. He was going forth into life armed with two pieces of information on dealing with loss:

1. Bury your feelings
2. Replace the loss

Now let's see how this information affected John in his next loss experience:

> "In 1958, my grandfather died. He was very important in my life—he was probably closer to me than my father was at that point. Every summer was spent at his farm. He taught me how to fish, hunt, and was the first to teach me how to play baseball.
>
> "When I was told he'd died, I was sitting in one of my high school classes. I can remember going numb. It was like being in a trance. After several minutes I began to cry and I suppose that made everyone uncomfortable. So they sent me to the principal's office so I could be by myself."

Since they didn't know what to do, they decided to send John to the office to be alone. This nonverbal yet powerful communication placed another piece of invalid information into his mind.

Meaning: Grieve alone.

> "Once again, I assumed the adults around me knew what they were doing. This attitude of handling pain alone was further reinforced when I got home that night. My mother was sitting in the living room with her head down and was obviously crying. As soon as I saw her, I wanted to go to her so we could cry together. Both my father and my uncle came and said to me:

> *"Don't disturb your mother. She'll be okay in a
> little while."*

Meaning: Grieve alone.

John now had three pieces of data on how to deal with
loss. He was soon to find out that not a single one of them
was going to be of any help to him:

> "I tried not to feel bad (remember, "Bury your
> feelings"), but you know and I know that I felt
> terrible. I wanted the adults to think I was doing
> okay, so I acted as if I was fine.
>
> "On those occasions when the pain was
> overwhelming, I'd go to my room and hide my
> feelings (remember, "Grieve alone"). That's what I
> thought I was supposed to do. Then came the
> major problem. It dawned on me that it wasn't
> going to be possible to replace my grandfather. We
> couldn't do what we'd done with the prior losses in
> my life (remember, "Replace the loss").
>
> "For over a year, each time I tried to drive
> down the road where my grandfather had lived, I
> couldn't do it. Every time I saw someone who
> resembled him, I'd cross the street or move away to
> avoid him. I still carried on conversations with him
> in my head; he came to me in my dreams. I
> couldn't stand to be around older people because I
> knew they'd die soon and leave me just like my
> grandfather.
>
> "I finally decided to talk to my father about
> what I was feeling. When I finished telling him, he
> said, "You're grieving, but you'll get over it.""

Meaning: Just give it time.

And there it was, the fourth piece of misinformation. That short phrase is probably responsible for more heartache than any other single factor in our society. The terrible part is, it isn't true. It's one of those falsehoods that's been passed down from generation to generation by ill-informed people.

We travel all over the United States and Canada training professionals and doing grief recovery seminars. In the course of doing this work we have come across countless grievers who've been told the same pieces of misinformation. All of this bad information causes massive pain. But the one that roots people into inaction more than any other is "Just give it time."

The mistaken idea that after enough time passes something will magically change to make us whole again is preposterous. If we were dealing with any other human pain, no one would say, "Just give it time."

If you came across a person with a broken arm or severe physical pain, you wouldn't say, "Just give it time." You'd get into action to help the person.

Since we know so little about pain to the human heart, since we know so little about grief, and since we don't want to admit to ignorance, we say: "Just give it time."

The sad part is, we come to believe it's true. People wait around for years with the idea that after a long enough period of time they will feel better again. Some of you reading this book already know this isn't true.

Recently in a seminar, we asked some people to raise their hands if they were still experiencing pain caused by a death that occurred more than twenty years ago. As expected, many people indicated this was true for them. They all believed that time would take care of the pain. We asked one woman if twenty years didn't seem like it might be a little long to be waiting for some recovery. She answered with a clear and classic statement: "Yes, it is, but I don't know what else to do."

Can you imagine the pain and frustration? The years of waiting for some relief? If you are a griever reading this book, not only can you imagine it, you know what it feels like.

WE'RE TAUGHT MYTHS ABOUT DEALING WITH THE PAST

In John's story about his grandfather he mentioned spending time on the farm and learning to fish, hunt, and play baseball. When reflecting on these times with his grandfather, he naturally wanted to relive these moments. This is the experience of reaching out for those who have always been there, only to find that when you need them one last time they are no longer there. Why do we feel the need to reach out for them? Because emotionally we're not yet ready to let our loved ones go. Why are we not yet ready? Because we're not yet emotionally complete with them. Why are we not complete with them yet? Because almost everything we have learned about dealing with loss works against us in terms of being emotionally complete with people.

When John was sent to the principal's office to be alone, it reinforced the fact that all of his life he'd been taught not to talk about his feelings. As John sat in the office and reflected on the relationship he had with his grandfather, he wanted to thank him one last time for all he had learned. This type of communication had scared him when his grandfather was alive. Since he'd been taught to put off until later doing things which scared him, he never communicated his feelings. Before "later" arrived, his grandfather died. Then he was caught in the trap of wishing he could change what happened. He began to feel extremely sad (indicating his emotional incompleteness) and frustrated by his desire for things to have been "DIFFERENT, BETTER, OR MORE."

Meaning: Regret the past.

Then John started to feel bad about himself and the choices he had made. Many people in our world mistakenly call this guilt. Wishing that things could somehow have been DIFFERENT, BETTER, OR MORE and feeling guilty are not the same. The truth is, all of us try to do the best we can with the tools we have. It's only upon hearing "You shouldn't feel guilty, you did the best you could do" that grievers begin to think in terms of guilt. This idea of guilt has become so prevalent that grievers often feel guilty if they smile or laugh.

This leads to another very sad situation for the griever. He or she then gets divorced from the fond memories of the loved one, which should be a help rather than a hindrance. Something reminds us of the loved one who died. Often this will lead to a fond memory. A fond memory will most times lead to happy feelings of reflection about the memory. If it stopped there, it would be fine. But it never seems to stop there. It continues on to some other memory, which leads to pain because we wish things were DIFFERENT, BETTER, OR MORE.

Many times people who are caught in this cycle will try to hold on to the fond memories. In grief recovery work, this is known as "enshrinement." Enshrinement is obsessively building memorials to the person who died. This is often demonstrated by keeping large numbers of objects around that represent the person. An example is the mother who had not changed one item in her daughter's room although her daughter had been dead for over five years. She had thought, "It's just too painful to confront the feelings of changing the things in her room."

Other people take on many of the character traits of the loved one; they may actually start to participate in some of the hobbies or even the careers of the deceased. When people do these things by choice, it's not a problem. But many times we do them unconsciously to get a kind of short-term relief from grief. Frank's father had spent his entire life as an electrical engineer working with computers. After his father's death Frank spent the next two years working in data processing. At the time he didn't see this as enshrinement, yet he never really knew why he left his chosen career in communications.

WE'RE TAUGHT MYTHS ABOUT DEALING WITH THE FUTURE

John's father was an alcoholic. When his father was intoxicated, he repeatedly spanked him for things he did not do:

> "Even though I would tell him it wasn't my
> fault, he didn't believe me and punished me
> anyway. It seemed very unfair to me and my faith
> in him was diminished."

What John was learning to expect was fear or betrayal.

Meaning: Don't trust.

Since the loss was never acknowledged or settled, his suspicion of adults expanded. He trusted less and was on guard more. This limited John's aliveness and freedom. It limited the type of people that he could have trusting relationships with. It caused him to be wary of all authority figures.

> "I'm not saying that this general loss of trust
> was right on my part. What I'm saying is, people
> don't like pain and so unconsciously they will try to
> avoid even the possibility of a repeat."

Loss of trust was painful, so John learned that the solution was "Don't trust," thereby eliminating the potential for pain.

When John's first girlfriend broke up with him, it reinforced the idea of not trusting people. From that point on he found he had great difficulty in trusting the girls he went out with. He was more tentative and held back since he didn't want to be hurt again. That limited his capacity for aliveness. We've all heard that relationships are supposed to be fifty-fifty. Of course it isn't true. For any relationship to work, it has to be 100 percent from both parties. What John kept doing was waiting for the other person to put in 50 percent first, while he held his 50 percent back in order to be safe. We know many grievers who have trouble starting up new relationships because they're afraid of the repeat of pain in the future.

Now, let's review what John had learned:

1. Bury your feelings

2. Replace the loss

3. Grieve alone

4. Just give it time

5. Regret the past (DIFFERENT, BETTER, OR MORE)

6. Don't trust

Not a very impressive list, is it? In fact, if John had continued to try to deal with loss using these tools any longer than he did, he'd probably be spiritually and emotionally numb.

WHY WE PERSIST IN BELIEVING THESE MYTHS

Why do we persist in trying to use information that hasn't worked for us? To understand why, you need to know some things about the computer we call the mind.

First, the mind only has access to what's been put into it. It cannot use what it doesn't know. If you are only given misinformation, that's all you have access to.

Secondly, the information stored in the mind is stored with importance attached. That means the more important the source of the information, the more tenaciously we believe it to be right. Most of the data John acquired about loss came from Mom and Dad. To a child, this is a very important source of information.

Thirdly, the mind's job is to believe that whatever it has stored in it is ALWAYS RIGHT! It's why people are so critical of each other. If you believe you're right and your friends don't agree with you, they're wrong! This is one of the reasons we're so critical of each other in our society and of those who are different from us. It's for these reasons that we persist in using misinformation in trying to process the feelings caused by loss. We believe that what we already know about loss is right.

The tools John was given are not unique. Almost everyone in our society has his or her own collection of tools that won't work. You have a list of inadequate and inappropriate tools as well. In Chapter 7, you'll have a chance to discover exactly what yours are.

None of the six pieces of information John learned about dealing with grief were true or helpful. They were all pieces of misinformation. But when misinformation is all we know, we think it's valid, and we continue to use it as if it will work to reduce our pain.

3

Others Are Ill-Prepared to Help Us Deal with Loss

In reading Chapter 2 you probably identified with some of the experiences described and recognized some of your own early life experiences in which you learned to process loss incorrectly. Everyone in our society has the same kind of inadequate and inappropriate information stored in the computer of his or her mind.

It is only natural and quite healthy for people who are caught in a grieving situation to seek solace from those around them. However, in rather short order it becomes abundantly clear to the griever that friends and associates are not of much help. Even though they are well meaning, they often say things that can seem inappropriate. How many times have we all thought to ourselves, "What should I say?"

THEY DON'T KNOW WHAT TO SAY

The problem is that many of the friends and professionals closest to us at the time of our grief have not experienced a significant emotional loss. Even if they have experienced significant loss, those closest to them did not know how to respond. Therefore, they have never learned what to do or say. If we remember our earlier example of society's response to first aid in dealing with physical pain compared to our response in dealing with emotional pain, it's easy to see how this lack of knowledge is perpetuated.

Let's say we have a friend who hurts his back. And let's say that this proves to be a physically painful event that we have no personal experience with. Yet we know someone who has had a similar injury that we can draw on in support of our friend. Perhaps we will tell our friend of this earlier situation and exactly what was done about it. We will verify the excruciating pain that a back injury can bring, and make real suggestions about recovery even though we have never had the experience ourselves. We will even refer him to a qualified professional in the community that specializes in recovery from back pain.

We actually make the pain resulting from a back injury okay for our friend to have. We know there's recovery from this pain through our personal knowledge, even though we have never had the experience ourselves. As a result of our friend's taking these suggestions on what to do about it, the pain is apt to clear. Where did we get these suggestions? From our own personal knowledge, *even though the experience wasn't ours.*

Now, let's say this pain resulted from a significant emotional loss. By the time we've completed childhood, all of us have experienced loss on some level. Yet did anyone know what to do about it? Did anyone even think that something needed to be done? For the most part, only those who were having the experience felt the need. When no real recovery suggestions are available, there is very little in our experience to share with others when it happens to them, and there is very little in their experience to share with us. Perhaps the best we really can do is to say, "Well, you know, it just takes time."

Since they have no other suggestions from previous experience, they actually proceed to encourage us how to "ACT recovered." This phenomenon has become so common that our next chapter is entirely devoted to it. This all perpetuates a fear of showing the feelings that result from emotional pain.

They're Afraid of Our Feelings

Very early on, society teaches us that feelings and the showing of feelings are somehow not appropriate. It starts with the admonition that "Big boys and girls don't cry." One can actually hear parents say, "Stop that crying or I'll give you a reason to cry."

Now, we don't want you to get the idea that parents are insensitive, because that isn't true. They could only pass on to their children what they were taught, and what they were taught was that feelings and the showing of feelings are not acceptable in society.

"Cry baby, cry baby" can be heard resounding around preschool playgrounds. This is proof that the lesson has already been learned by age four or five.

As children we can remember seeing lots of cowboy movies. In one film a certain cowboy had a great affinity for his horse, named Paint. About halfway into the film, Paint breaks a leg. The cowboy just can't believe it. He pulls out his trusty six-shooter and shoots Paint in the head. He then blows the smoke off the barrel of his gun, twirls it back into his holster, and walks away as if nothing's happened. Having to shoot your favorite horse that you've loved for years wouldn't be painful for this cowboy—he was a real man.

That's exactly what we learned from this image. For centuries the majesty of kings and queens alike has taught us that greatness means showing no sign of upset.

"Get a hold of yourself."
"You can't fall apart."
"Keep a stiff upper lip."
"Pull yourself up by the bootstraps."
"Be strong for the children."

This is only a small sample of the statements heard on a daily basis expressing the fear others have about us showing our feelings. As a society we're uncomfortable when confronted by displays of painful emotion. This is what causes listeners to change the subject.

THEY TRY TO CHANGE THE SUBJECT

If you can remember trying to tell someone how you were feeling, recall how the listener wanted to look interested and at the earliest opportunity said, "Gosh, that really must be tough—by the way, did you hear about Sally?"

Let's break this "changing of the subject" down and look at what really happens. Here is an example of an

occasion when the griever has to talk with his friend about
the loss:

FRIEND: Hi. Are you okay?

GRIEVER: Yes, it's just real hard.

FRIEND: When did you find out?

GRIEVER: This morning. The hospital called. I just
couldn't believe it . . .

At this point the griever is weeping, trying to think of how
to say what it is he's feeling. Meanwhile the friend is quite
uncomfortable during this period of silence, and before
the griever has a chance to continue, the friend says,
"Well, everything's going to be okay. Oh look, I can't
believe that Joe stopped by. Hi, Joe . . ."

Now, this really is a good friend of the griever's. His
listening skills are no better or worse than those of most
people in this situation. Usually the problem is they just
aren't silent long enough for the griever to respond any
further. Very rarely does anyone take the time to truly
listen to the feelings the griever is trying to express.

Rarely do we hear:

"Could you tell me about it?"

"What happened?"

"I can't imagine how painful this must be."

"How did you find out?"

"What was your relationship like."

or, simply:

"I'm so sorry."

If we did hear some of these comments, it was seldom that the listeners payed attention long enough to express an honest desire to hear our responses. Perhaps they would give us a hug and say, "Did you see the cookies I brought?" "What beautiful flowers your Aunt Mabel sent," or, "Did she have any life-insurance policies?"

This change-the-subject attitude was recently displayed on the ABC Television program "20/20," in a show about grief caused by the death of a pet.

The program was really well done and was very sensitive to a griever's feelings. When the segment was over, the camera shifted back to Hugh Downs and Barbara Walters. Barbara Walters had started to get tears in her eyes. The final sentence spoken prior to the commercial came from Barbara Walters. She said, "Before I cry, let's change the subject."

So, the clear message to viewers was that showing feelings is not acceptable. The clear message was:

"Let's deal with our feelings by changing the subject."

They Intellectualize

One of the reasons this attitude prevails is the major amount of importance that we place on our intellect. That's not to say there is anything wrong with using our minds, but where is it written that we can't employ both the gifts of intellect and of emotions when they're called for? One of humanity's great gifts is our ability to show emotion. Yet society seems to place negative value on this gift.

Our reliance on intellect at the expense of showing feelings has reached epidemic proportions. This is particularly true where grief is concerned. In part, this is because the death of a loved one is not an everyday occurrence. If statistics are to be believed, we will each have the death of a loved one occur every nine to thirteen years. Even when combined with other significant emotional losses, major grief experiences occur so infrequently that we never really get familiar with what the experience is like. Because of our lack of personal knowledge, we continue the habit of dealing with loss based on misinformation. This habit can only lead to the unsuccessful conclusion of grief events, or emotional incompleteness.

It is not surprising that many people try to deal with their pain by using their intellect rather than expressing their feelings. Since we rely on intellect on a daily basis, we're far more practiced at employing its use.

Based on the informal surveys we conduct at each of our seminars, we would expect that more than four out of five reactions you heard following the loss of a loved one implied that you shouldn't deal with the feelings you were experiencing. The things you heard were probably an appeal to the intellect. I hope you don't think we're exaggerating this point. There have been research studies done concerning common statements heard by grievers very shortly after a death. Many common sentences have been identified and they can be divided into two major categories: (1) Those that were helpful in talking about feelings, and (2) those that were an appeal to intellect or fell into the category of advice, such as:

"We understand how you feel."

"Be thankful you have another son."

"It's over now, let's not deal with it."

"The living must go on."

"Get it together, now."

"Snap out of it."

"All things must pass."

"She led a full life."

"You'll find somebody else."

"You must be strong."

"God will never give you more than you can handle."

"It's just going to take some time."

These are all comments that we ourselves as grievers have heard. Since the griever is experiencing intense emotional suffering, which has very little to do with the griever's intellect, the statements seem quite inappropriate.

They Think That Keeping "Busy" Helps

"You must keep busy."

This is one of those statements that we're conditioned to believe very early. The idea is, if we just keep active, we'll somehow begin to feel better. It works for about five-minute intervals, if we're lucky. The suggestion only helps us to avoid the real issues, which makes the pain last longer.

A few years ago we were talking to a waitress in Dallas,

Texas. She told us that waitressing was one of three part-time jobs she had. We asked her when she found time to sleep. As soon as we asked, she sat down and tears came to her eyes. "I've had trouble sleeping for over three years now." She went on to tell us that since her husband died, sleep was difficult for her. When she told her friends about it, they all said, "You must keep active."

So she'd been keeping busy for more than three years. This wasn't helping her to sleep any better; she came home at night so tired she'd pass out from exhaustion. Passing out from exhaustion and getting restful sleep are not the same thing. But she didn't know any better, so she followed the advice of people who thought they were helping her. She was so tired and in such pain. We told her who we were and asked if we could help her. She said, "No, it's only been three years."

We could hear the hope in her voice. If she could just hang on for a while longer, then something would happen and she'd feel better.

If enough time goes by, she'll become so familiar with her pain that she'll establish a new identity around it. She will truly develop a relationship with her pain.

THEY DON'T WANT TO TALK ABOUT DEATH

It's gotten to such an extreme that those around us can't even say the word "death." Think about it:

"She passed away."

"He's gone to his eternal rest."

"Dad's gone."

"He expired."

"We've lost Mother."

Think about how all this sounds to small children. They ask questions, expecting to hear truthful answers.

"What happened to Grandpa?"

"Grandpa's gone to sleep."

The child takes one look at Grandpa and knows something isn't quite right about that answer. He's confused but assumes he's been told the truth. There must be two types of sleep. So he then spends the next six months being afraid to go to sleep at night.

We're sorry to say this, but God has been given a bad name where children are concerned.

"What happened to my daddy?"

"God has called him home."

For the next several years, the child is upset and confused by God. Don't you think it might be more appropriate to tell the child what her parents believe to be the truth—"Your dad has died and after he died, he went to be with God."?

They Want Us to Keep Our Faith

When John's brother died, he was told, "You shouldn't be angry with God."

Now, John knew he shouldn't be angry with God, but the truth was he was really steamed at God. No one knew to tell him that anger at God is an almost automatic and normal response to the death of a loved one. We've relied on intellect for years, so we search for understandable reasons for events. When we can't find one, we still feel the need to assign blame. God is a convenient place to assign blame. Through our own personal experience we're convinced that God is big enough to understand our shortcomings.

This anger will pass if we're allowed to express the feelings. We have to be able to tell someone that we're angry with God, and not be judged for it or told we're bad because of it. If not, this anger may persist forever and block spiritual growth. We've watched people never return to their religion because they weren't allowed to express their true feelings. If this happens, the griever is cut off from one of the most powerful support resources he or she might have.

THEY WANT THEIR HELP TO BE EFFECTIVE

Even after having been through countless losses of friends and loved ones, when we tried to talk to someone who had experienced a death, we fell into the same traps, or said the same kinds of things. Every griever we've ever talked to wants to help other grievers. Invariably, they find that they say the wrong things.

This is true of the professional community as well. No one seems to know whose job this is. In many communities we have access to marriage counselors, child development counselors, alcohol and drug abuse counselors, counseling for eating disorders, financial counselors. Each one of these professionals has a clearly defined set of communication tools to apply to every personal situation in order to point the way for recovery. Until recently, this set of tools has not been available in the area of bereavement.

We know because we've trained many of these professionals. As the years go by, we are finding that more and more of these caring people are acquiring these communication skills. They are attending seminars to learn how to be the grief recovery educators in their community. They are learning specifically how to talk to grievers about grief and how to be of better service.

Our experience has shown us that communities want the role of grief recovery counselor to be filled. Our seminars are attended by health-care professionals from all areas (doctors, nurses, clergy, etc.), yet the majority of professionals attending our seminars are funeral directors and cemeterians. Not once in their standard professional training are these people given more than three hours of classroom credit for learning how to communicate with the bereaved. They are taught embalming, state disposition laws, health codes, business administration, inventory control. Yet not once are they taught specifics about what to do with the pain of grief. They have literally been starved for further knowledge by a society that does not actively pursue awareness in the area of grief recovery.

We have found funeral and cemetery people, who are constantly confronted with the pain of the bereaved, to be the group most compassionate and willing to learn. We know that given the right tools, these individuals have the greatest care-giving potential in the community—no matter how large or small that community is.

We all want the support we give and the support

given to us to be effective. In all of our travels and experiences, we know that people just want to love and be loved. This means improving our ability to communicate the truth about our feelings. Never will our skill to communicate the truth be perfected, yet the better we get at it, the better we feel.

Recovery is about feeling good. This step-by-step program will absolutely improve your ability to communicate the truth. This is the most you can do to give and get support with grief. By bringing this awareness to yourself, you will also be able to pass it on to others.

4

"Academy Award" Recovery

In the last chapter, we discussed the ways in which society literally teaches us how to "ACT recovered." Understanding this phase of grief is enormously important. A false image of recovery is the most common obstacle all grievers must overcome if they expect to move beyond their loss. "ACADEMY AWARD" Recovery is its name. It could also be called the "I'M FINE" phase, the "PUT ON YOUR HAPPY FACE" phase, the "BE FINE FOR MY FAMILY AND FRIENDS" phase, or the "I WANT TO HELP GRIEVERS" phase. You might sit down and ask yourself how many of these "ACT recovered" faces you're currently using. Most of you already know what we're talking about.

In the previous chapter, we discussed how others respond to a griever at the time of a loss. We showed how the vast majority of verbal and nonverbal communications a griever will hear are appeals to the intellect and do not encourage the expression of feelings. Such intellectualizing actually increases a griever's sense of isolation instead of having the intended result of reducing it. It creates a feeling of being judged, evaluated, and advised. In a relatively short time, the griever discovers that he or she must actually "ACT recovered" in order to be treated in an acceptable manner.

WE WANT THE APPROVAL OF OTHERS

We all like praise and compliments. We all like approval. We've all laughed at jokes that are off-color. We've all agreed with things we didn't really believe in order to feel a part of a group. This has been learned as part of early childhood training and has been reinforced to the point of obsession.

So when 80 percent of all the comments we hear tell us to behave in a certain way, what happens is . . . we behave that way.

Normally, the scenario goes like this: The griever, who is experiencing the most painful situation he or she has ever had, takes a chance and mentions a feeling he is having. The listener, who is afraid of the expression of strong feelings, will sometimes try to acknowledge the feeling quickly and then offer some intellectual or logical advice.

When Frank's father died, a friend called and asked him, "How are you doing? Are you doing okay?"

Frank said, "I'm sad. I feel real sad."

His friend then responded by saying, "You shouldn't feel sad, you should be grateful. He accomplished so much during his life, it was just his time to go."

On an intellectual level he was right, and at that time Frank wanted his friend's approval. However, his friend's comment didn't help him feel any better. In fact, what he wanted to do was scream at his friend that there was a lot more his father wanted to do in life and he hadn't just gone, he was dead!

When John's infant son died, it tore him apart; but what he heard were things such as:

> *"You and your wife should be grateful that you can have other children."*
>
> *"It was just not meant to be."*
>
> *"You're strong enough to handle it."*

While on an intellectual basis all these statements are true, they still didn't help John to deal with his feelings. Yet John knew that he didn't want to be alone. The question was, how could he honestly share his feelings without driving listeners away?

Because we want the approval of those around us and because we are tired of feeling bad, we opt for "ACADEMY AWARD" Recovery and begin to "ACT recovered" even though we're not. And our performances are so good we're likely to convince ourselves as well as others that we really are all right.

Through our work with grievers around the country, we get to see some of the most "put-together" people on earth. They look good, they sound good, and they even try to convince us they are feeling good. When we meet people who've just experienced a loss, we ask them how they're doing. Invariably, the answer is the same: "I'm fine."

It's no wonder so many people opt for acting as if they're doing fine. They project an attitude of: "What's done is done, I can't do anything about it, so I'm getting on with my life."

But can they really? We think not! Only alone at home, hidden from family and friends, can they cry and show the enormous pain they still feel.

THOSE WHO WANT TO HELP GRIEVERS

"ACADEMY AWARD" Recovery is also the phase when many people become convinced that they're truly ready and interested in helping other grievers. And the truth about these people is that they DO want to help grievers.

It's just that most people who are motivated to help grievers are in fact grieving themselves and are emotionally incomplete with a previous loss. Even though you may not be consciously aware of this, it is nevertheless true. So, if you fall into this category, don't skip ahead, just do the same work that the griever is asked to do in the following chapters. In this way, you'll also learn how to help others.

Before you can help anyone else, you must have resolved the grief episodes in your own life.

WE EXPERIENCE A LOSS OF ALIVENESS

This kind of false recovery can lead to a loss of aliveness and spontaneity which is almost impossible to overcome. Many people fall into a trap of quiet desperation, sometimes feeling good, sometimes feeling bad, but never being able to return to a state of full happiness and joy.

When Frank was seven years old his family went on a vacation to Disneyland. He'll never forget the excitement of that day:

> "I remember the book of tickets for all the rides they had. There were A,B,C,D, and E tickets in my book. The E ticket rides were the best. I remember my grandmother felt too old to use hers and gave them all to me. It felt like all my dreams had come true. Life couldn't get any better than this. I thought it would stay that way forever. Six months later, my grandmother died. It would be many years before I'd reclaim the happiness, joy, and freedom I had that day."

Stop now for a moment and think back to your childhood. Life was going to be a happy, joyous, and wonderful thing. But slowly, due to many small, unresolved losses, we woke up one day to find that life just had not worked out the way we thought it would.

The price we pay for the misinformation we have about dealing with loss is too great. Each time a loss is not concluded there is cumulative restriction on our aliveness. Life becomes something to endure; the world seems like a hostile place in which to live. The problem is we never had a fair chance at dealing with the loss events in our lives. It's like trying to pound nails without knowing about hammers.

Recently a funeral director at one of our seminars shared this story with us. A man had died, and during the visiting hours at the funeral home his grandson had come to see his body. The boy was standing by the casket, crying. His grandmother came over and the funeral director heard her say, "Don't cry, Jimmy. Each tear you cry drowns one of God's angels."

If it weren't so sad it would be a comedy. The saddest part of this story is that a whole new generation of young people are being given the same type of misinformation we were given. Sure, they laugh once in a while, but if you listen very carefully you'll always hear the crying underneath. It gets to the point where they just want to be alone. We know a man whose wife of forty years died. For several weeks after the funeral, people called and stopped by his house to visit. He was in a lot of pain, as you can imagine, and talked openly about his feelings during these weeks.

All his friends seemed to be uncomfortable when he discussed his loss. In fact, they seemed to be uncomfortable because they *were* uncomfortable. Soon they stopped calling and stopping by to visit. He began to ask his friends why they didn't call any more. They told him they were calling but he must not be home. Now he knew that he'd rarely been out of the house, but his friends persisted in saying that they were still calling. Soon he began to think that perhaps he wasn't hearing the phone or wasn't remembering when he left the house, so he bought a telephone answering machine. Every time he left the house, he made a specific effort to turn on the machine.

He discovered that no one was calling. He was unconsciously being isolated by those he looked to for support. They were unconsciously directing him to ACT recovered.

At the same time he was growing tired of feeling sad and in pain. So he tried to get into positive thinking and to act as if he were in better shape than he really was.

But inside he continued to suffer. Eventually he sought help. At that time he had gone to the only available source he could think of that had not evaluated him for the feelings he was having—the local funeral home that had buried his wife. The staff convinced the man to attend a weekend seminar for grievers we were conducting nearby.

He participated in the same step-by-step program laid out in this book. Here's what happened:

> "The seminar literally saved my life. I had given up the will to live and was doing all the classic 'no-no's': isolating, self-guilt, living only in the past, thinking, 'If only I had BEEN DIFFERENT, BETTER, OR MORE.'
>
> "I learned that others had the same feelings and I was not the only apple on the tree. I learned that I had been carrying a deep guilt over my father's death thirty-five years before, as well as my mother's death over twelve years before. I thought the death of my wife was the beginning and end of everything I was and was not feeling.
>
> "Through this program I was able to participate in my own life again. I discovered the joy of a safe place, a hug, and a smile. I found an inner happiness that I had never before experienced."

But before this person took action and began our program, he was extremely practiced in the process of acting well and isolating himself. He had stopped talking about his real feelings and begun to bottle them up. A crisis was pending.

WE SUPPRESS OUR FEELINGS

When we bottle up feelings caused by loss, it is the same as starting the timer of a time bomb. In the beginning, the bomb ticks softly. The ticks represent problems which are experienced by grievers who don't know how to successfully grieve. It's as if each one of these signs of trouble are ticks of the bomb progressively getting closer to exploding:

1. Sleeplessness—Please be honest with yourself and ask yourself if you're still experiencing sleep difficulty.

2. Periods of confusion—Over making even simple decisions. Things that before the loss would not have bewildered us at all are now unclear, painful, and confusing.

3. Things that aren't there—Many people still find themselves hearing a familiar sound and then going to look for the person who died. Many people still spend time talking to the person who died, setting a place for them at the dinner table, and so forth.

4. Behavioral disorders—Falling into the trap of taking prescription medication, consuming alcohol, or developing an eating disorder to dull the pain.

5. Fear—Of the future and fear of the past, as shown by second-guessing our decisions since the death.

6. Isolation—Many people find themselves emotionally withdrawn from the world. They have small outbursts of anger and can't understand why. Through isolation they move further into their protective shell, away from the very feelings they must confront in order to recover.

We Act Out

The longer the time bomb ticks, the closer it comes to an explosion. The same is true for a griever. The longer a person bottles up the feelings caused by the loss, the closer he or she comes to some serious and detrimental consequences. Sometimes these consequences are hard to understand—events like senseless massacres in post offices, restaurants, and other public places. But not all situations have this kind of shock value. Not long ago several articles appeared about the suicide rate among grievers. There are countless cases of child abuse which can be directly traced to the prior death of another child. And, as might be expected, the divorce rate in child-loss marriages is extremely high.

Recently, a major magazine had an excerpt from a celebrity's autobiography. The article described several significant emotional losses in her life and how she developed behavioral disorders, including a problem with food. Her exact quote on the cover of the magazine was: "It's a wonder I didn't explode!"

And in typical Hollywood style, an account of a recent local tragedy told of a young "All-American" girl who had hitchhiked from her hometown to find fame and fortune as a star. Within the next nine months she participated in a lifestyle that neither she nor her family had ever thought possible and then committed suicide through a drug overdose.

While putting the article together, the reporter went back to the girl's hometown to interview her mother. Hidden away in the bottom corner of the last page of the article was a quote from her mom that said: "She just wasn't the same after her grandfather died." How can we diffuse this time bomb?

STARTING TO RECOVER

You've already made several correct choices regarding your need to acquire a new skill, although perhaps you didn't know it:

- You have acknowledged that a problem exists.
- You have acknowledged that the problem is associated with loss.
- You have acknowledged by your action of reading this handbook that you are now willing to deal with your grief.

The next three chapters will introduce you to the first steps, or components, necessary for moving beyond loss. The remainder of the book will take a detailed look at these five stages and their implementation. Success in expediting your process of moving through grief will depend on your willingness to follow through on each step along the way.

PART TWO

Preparing for Change

5

Choosing to Recover

Procrastination—putting off doing things that we're afraid of doing—is a favorite practice for everybody. We live with an attitude that there will always be time in the future to take care of the things we could handle now. Rationalization is our favorite tool. Then someone dies and we feel as if it's too late. Over time, we begin to make the death or other loss responsible for how badly we're feeling. As long as we believe that someone or something else is responsible, then we're helpless to recover.

WHO IS RESPONSIBLE?

After recognizing the fallacy of the belief that "Grief just takes time," the next most difficult hurdle for grievers to overcome is the lifelong incorrect belief that other people or events are responsible for their feelings.

All of us have a tendency to say:

" 'So-and-so' made me angry."
" 'So-and-so' ruined my day."

"I'd be okay if 'So-and-so' hadn't done 'such-and-such' to me."

This attitude of nonresponsibility for our feelings and our actions is rampant. It seems to be one of society's favorite pastimes.

This, too, starts with early "influence learning." Mom says to the child, "You make me happy."

Dad says, "You make me proud."

Soon the child gets the mistaken idea that he is responsible for how his parents are feeling. As the child grows, he imitates what he sees demonstrated around him. Before long the child comes home from school and announces, "My friend Bobby at school really makes me angry."

This is where and how the cycle begins. We've often used a story to illustrate this concept. We call it "The on-the-Way-to-Work-in-the-Car Story":

One morning a man is on his way to work in his car. He comes to a red light and, being a law-abiding person, he stops. Sitting at the light, he begins to daydream—he is off on one of those rocket rides in his head that we all go on from time to time. Meanwhile, the light changes from red to green.

Our friend doesn't see the light change; the driver in the car behind him does. When our friend's car doesn't move, the guy behind him sounds his horn to notify him that the light has turned green. Our friend then rolls down his window and thanks the guy behind him for honking at him and calling his attention to the fact that the light has changed.

Whom are we kidding here? We all know that it goes more like this:

Our friend becomes embarrassed. No one likes to feel embarrassed. He sure doesn't want to be responsible for causing his own embarrassment. He, too, has a lifetime's practice of making others responsible for his feelings. So, instead of saying thank you to the driver for calling his attention to the fact that the light has changed, he thinks: "Boy, that guy makes me mad!"

Almost at once his mind becomes filled with plans and schemes to save face or get even. He rolls down his window, puts his head out, and does exactly what he learned in that self-help seminar he attended two years before. He reports his feelings: "Hey, buddy, get off my back!"

He then proceeds to drive a little bit slower in front of this guy in order to punish him for ruining his day. He knows he's right about this one!

Our friend is angry and upset and cannot see that he is the architect of his own discomfort. He doesn't acknowledge that he is indeed responsible for the feelings that result from his attitudes and actions. What ruins the picnic—is it the rain or one's attitude toward the rain?

Some people are ready to believe that a late bus is the result of a conspiracy. Others think that the government is ruining their lives, or that the boss is the cause of their misery. But what this all boils down to is the belief that *"They* make me angry." This leads to an almost automatic critical response toward anyone or anything we misperceive as being responsible for our feelings. We become expert at *other*-examination rather than *self*-examination.

When we make other people responsible for our feelings, we also make them responsible for ending our feelings. When we make loss totally responsible for our pain, we make replacement of the loss [an impossibility, as we learned in Chapter 2] *our only hope for ending the pain.*

Keep in mind, all the things talked about so far operate together. That is to say:

1. If we believe that the loss is the total cause of how we feel, and

2. Everyone around us says it just takes time, then

3. We're left with no hope other than time.

But, as it must by now be clear, time won't do anything but pass, unless you take responsibility for your own recovery. For now, that means continuing to turn the pages and find a solution.

Choosing the New Path

So far we have said:

• Neither this handbook nor any other guide or counselor can recover you from grief.

• Only you can recover yourself.

• With the step-by-step program laid out here, recovery need not take as long as you have perhaps thought it would.

For the present, look at this program as a game plan. Game plans are predefined programs of action designed to achieve a desired goal. In order for game plans to work, they must have parameters, also known as rules. This program, like all other effective game plans, has its rules, and in order for us to agree to the first rule of the game, we must understand who is responsible for our feelings and the actions we take as a result of those feelings.

Many times in our seminars we will compare this portion of our game plan with the game of Monopoly. Since many of us are familiar with this game, it makes a good analogy. When Parker Brothers first designed their game, the rules stated that if you landed on a piece of property for sale by the bank (not yet bought by any other player), you were obligated to either buy it or offer it up for auction. In either case, the game could not continue until the ownership of that property was settled. It's quite simple to see why they felt this rule necessary. The game works better. This rule shows us how the value of real estate is affected by the economic conditions of all the other players. It is truly a much more interesting game when you take responsibility to be aware of and play by the originally designed rules. So the real answer to why the rules exist in any game plan is because it works better.

There are many components to the game of Monopoly: the rules, the players, the board, the dice, Chance and Community Chest cards, even the table or floor you choose to play on. Each person gets a game piece. You choose a banker that distributes the money and keeps track of property ownership. Each component is necessary down to the instructions on the inside of the box top. The game won't work without each one of these components working in harmony. Yet no one of these components is responsible for the satisfaction you get from playing the game. No one of these components is responsible for your winning or losing. It's not the game; it's not the person who taught you the game; it's not whether you're the Scotty Dog, the Old Shoe, or the Top Hat marker; nor is it necessarily who you play the game with that gives you your experience—it is YOUR PARTICIPATION in the game that dictates the experience you have. The same reasoning applies to the steps laid out in this handbook. They are here to increase your participation. They exist because we know through our experience that the program will not work without them.

STEP ONE: FINDING A PARTNER

Your steps will begin with finding a partner. Just as you cannot play Monopoly without a game board,

YOU CANNOT RECOVER ALONE!

In a very short time following the death of a loved one, people tend to detach from their feelings. Detaching from our feelings leads to isolation. It's this isolation which makes recovery impossible. In order to make recovery possible you're going to have to choose a new path. You're going to have to find someone with whom to participate. You're going to have to find and establish a grief recovery partnership.

You may not want to do this. You may feel that no one really understands the pain you're in. You may feel that even your own friends don't really comprehend your sorrow.

When people say they understand, they really can't. They didn't have the same relationship that you had. Grief is caused by the end of a relationship. Your relationship was personal and distinct, therefore your grief is personal and distinct. Even other family members had their own special relationships and they were different from yours; therefore their feelings are different from yours. Each person experiences his or her pain at 100 percent. It makes no sense to compare your pain with someone else's. It makes no sense for someone else to attempt to understand yours. If others have shown intolerance or impatience for your pain, try to forgive them and try not to be impatient with or intolerant of theirs.

Due to a common lack of patience and tolerance of a griever's pain, it is natural for grievers to be told to seek others who have experienced a similar loss. Widows are told they can only relate to widows; parents who have lost children are told they can only relate to other such parents. Fortunately for those who participate in our Outreach Programs, this conclusion is false. We have found that anyone who has suffered intense emotional loss has expanded patience and tolerance for another's grief.

No matter how convinced you might be that no one can understand or help, it is imperative that you have support. While your pain is your own, you must find a fellow griever so you can learn and recover together as partners. It won't be hard. Almost everyone in our society is not finished with some grief event. As a matter of fact, if there's someone standing to your left or right, you're probably looking at another griever who could qualify as your partner.

There are over 2 million deaths per year in the United States alone. (Keep in mind, we're only talking about grief caused by death. People grieve for many other losses. Job change, retirement, moving, and divorce are only a small sample of other things all of us grieve over.) For each death there are an average of three close friends or relatives who experience significant pain. That's 6 million new grievers each year.

Unresolved grief can last a lifetime. So take 6 million new grievers per year and multiply by any number of prior years and you can start to see the magnitude of the problem. You can also see just how many people who are potential grief recovery partners.

It may be that another family member of yours is grieving over the same death. If you haven't clearly expressed how you're feeling, he or she may not know. You may already have a built-in partner for your recovery work in your own family.

If not, there are countless places to look for such a new friend. At work you've heard people talk about someone who died. Your local health club, the grocery store, the drugstore, and your church are all places you can find another griever. If you really want to be brave, bring up the topic of grief at a social gathering. Sooner or later, most likely later, someone will talk honestly with you.

When you do find potential partners, be honest with them. Show them this book and tell them what you plan to do. Ask if they're tired of hurting, too. See if they're willing to recover with you. Don't be discouraged if several choose not to. You'll hear all kinds of excuses. Just keep looking until you're successful. We know one griever who acquired a copy of this book from a local funeral home. After reading this section of the handbook, the griever called the funeral director and described the problem of not being able to find a partner. This griever ended up in a partnership with three other grievers.

There's a chance that you'll find more than one partner, too. This is fine and can work quite well, although we suggest keeping the size of your group down to five or six. Otherwise, the meetings you'll have with one another could last too long. For the sake of clarity, instructions to the steps we'll be presenting throughout the rest of the handbook assume there are only two of you.

STEP TWO: MAKING A COMMITMENT

Once you've found this friend, you both must make several mutual commitments. These commitments are an extension of the rules to this program, without which the program will not work. The commitments will make it possible for you to feel secure enough to do the work that must be done.

The commitments are:

1. TOTAL HONESTY

2. ABSOLUTE CONFIDENTIALITY

Together you must create a safe, loving, nonjudgmental environment in which to work. Together you must do the best you can to maintain such an environment. These mutual assurances are essential for you both.

TOTAL HONESTY　When we say TOTAL HONESTY, we mean honesty to the best of your ability about your feelings and about the loss events in your life. Your ability to see and therefore tell the truth about these things will improve as you continue to work in this program.

In no way are we assuming that you, the reader, are a dishonest person. We're asking for this commitment between you and your partner because, without a willing-ness for total disclosure about the loss events in your lives, you cannot recover from them. For some of you there are things from the past that you have perhaps never told anyone. Earlier we said that recovery is claiming our cir-cumstances instead of our circumstances claiming us. When you're totally honest with yourself, you'll see that your secrets are truths about yourself that you find impos-sible to accept. There is no way to discover a new reality about your life without first accepting the truth about the past.

Not all of us have skeletons in our closets. Yet now is the time to begin to be honest with yourself about whether you belong in this category. As authors of this book, both of us have belonged in this category at one time or another. Here's an example that Frank will share with you:

"First you need to know a little about the family I came from. We lived in southeastern Texas in a very middle-class, white Anglo-Saxon Protestant community—sometimes known as WASP. You truly could not find a more 'All-American' family, which is perhaps not the healthiest family to come from—it just wasn't abnormal. I was the baby of the family, with one sister five years older than me. My father taught college his entire life and my sister became quite the scholar everyone seemed to expect from my family's reputation.

"I, too, was attempting to follow in these footsteps while attending the University of Texas at

Austin, but I was doing so with quite a resentment toward an old and ongoing breakdown in communications with my father.

"In my sophomore year, at the age of nineteen, I had a 'falling out' with my father over what to study and where to do it. I was determined to move to New York and pursue a career in acting and communications. I left the family, school, and everything that I had come to call home; went to New York City; supported myself as a cab driver; continued to pursue my education; and participated in a lifestyle completely opposite to the one I had grown up with.

"To make a long and confused story short, what began as fast and liberated living became, within two years, a serious drug addiction. Having had very little contact with my family during this time, I received a phone call one night from my sister informing me that my father had died suddenly of a massive heart attack at the age of fifty-nine.

"There is no time here to discuss the many conflicting thoughts, feelings, and actions that resulted from this news. I will say that when I went home to arrange my father's funeral, I knew there was no way anyone from my past could ever find out about the nature of my lifestyle. At that time there was no way I could let anyone know about my drug addiction. This was my secret. Not only was I not willing to tell anyone, but making such a confession never even existed as an option for me. Having had such a realistic view of my family and the background I had come from, it couldn't occur to me because this truth was totally unacceptable. While in Texas, it was impossible for me to accept the reality of my life in New York.

"It would be three long and stress-filled years before I would be completely aware of who I had become prior to my father's death. At that point I was able to tell my secret, but not yet willing. The willingness didn't come for two more years. I always thought there would be time later to straighten these things out. Never did it occur to me he would die so soon."

In disclosing this and many other truths about ourselves, we have grown to realize that most people, at one time or another, have had to be honest about things they'd rather not have to admit to. If you're waiting for someone to go first, Frank just did it for you. Your willingness to consider this kind of TOTAL HONESTY will prove to be vital to your recovery.

There are lots of other ways to be dishonest. Dishonesty by omission and broad mental reservations are only two examples. Often people tell the truth as far as it goes but they withhold information if they think disclosing it will make them look bad. How many times have you told a story to someone and during the process "fudged" on being totally honest about a few minor details or exaggerated a few details to make you and the story sound better? If at any time while working with your partner you catch yourself doing this, stop and recommit yourself to TOTAL HONESTY. Remember, if you are not totally honest to the best of your ability, if you only give your recovery a halfhearted attempt, this program will not work.

ABSOLUTE CONFIDENTIALITY During the course of the work you must do, you're going to talk about emotionally painful events and circumstances in your life with your partner. "ABSOLUTE CONFIDENTIALITY" means you carry any personal or painful information your partner has shared to the grave with you. "ABSOLUTE CONFIDENTIALITY" means you trust your partner to do the same. It means that wherever you choose to share, these intimacies and personal events must also be a safe place for both of you. It means that whatever you share in that place must remain in that place. It means that you must never breach your partner's confidence.

Death and reactions to death are the most off-limits topics for discussion in our society. Since few people know very much about grief, the two of you working together must create your own support system. This support system cannot operate without integrity. It is imperative that you inform your partner at the earliest opportunity when you must be late or must cancel a meeting. If you have a history of being habitually tardy, use this step-by-step program as a chance to break that habit. Making a strong commitment to punctuality will give your partnership confidence. These commitments are essential for your support system. Be sure you talk about them in depth. Don't give your word unless you're willing to back it up with action.

STEP THREE: REVIEWING CHAPTERS 1 TO 4

Once you've made the commitments verbally between you and your partner, it's time to go to work. This step is especially designed for those of you who buy hand-books, skip through the pages looking for the exercises, and proceed to follow the instructions for solving your problem. It's quite all right if you are one of these people. We understand and truly regard this action as an honest effort to recover. For some problems this method actually works. Yet, it never works as well as being thorough and reading the rest of the handbook. It simply will not work at all for recovery from grief.

Begin this step by agreeing on a time frame that will allow each of you to read or reread on your own the first four chapters of this handbook. During this reading make notes and underline things that you agree and disagree with. Note things that you relate to from your own experience. Be clear, since you'll want to discuss these things with your partner.

STEP FOUR: YOUR FIRST MEETING

When this reading is done, you will have your first "support group" meeting with your partner. Don't delay or be vague about setting the date and time. Be very specific and clear as to exactly where and when you'll meet. Don't just say, "Let's get together next week"; that's far too indefinite. Be very precise about time, date, and location. Remember your commitment to punctuality. Don't give your mind a chance to put off your decision to recover. Procrastination is never a very good idea; where grief recovery is concerned, it can root you into not taking action at all. Being specific is just one of the small correct actions that you have to make.

The following is a checklist for this meeting between you and your partner. Be sure to allow yourselves enough time to cover each of these topics fully. An hour and a half should do it.

1. Discuss the things you identified with in your reading of the first four chapters. Give yourselves a good half hour to have this discussion. Go over your notes together. See how similar your experiences were as grievers. You're going to be amazed at how much you have in common.

2. Read this chapter together. Alternate your reading. You read two paragraphs and your partner reads two paragraphs. Stop along the way to clarify and discuss your common and unique experiences. Be sure each of you is clear about who is responsible for your own attitudes, feelings, actions, and ultimate recovery.

3. Take time in reaffirming your commitments to TOTAL HONESTY and ABSOLUTE CONFIDENTIALITY.

4. Plan your next meeting. Once again, set an exact date, time, and location. We strongly suggest you make each meeting within a week of your last one, but at least a day later. You'll need enough time on your own to read the next step and do the work indicated there. During this time between meetings, you'll also want to reflect on how your last meeting went and adjust to the relationship as it evolves between you and your partner. Sometimes being this honest this quickly in a new relationship can cause much apprehension. Be sure not to sec-

ond-guess your decision to do this work. Stay committed to your recovery. Most of the time, thinking you have the wrong partner is just another excuse for not doing the work.

5. Do not end this meeting feeling incomplete. You must feel that you and your partner are committed to each other's recovery. You'll find that what you might not do for yourself alone, you will accomplish within your commitment to your partner.

There will be many other steps, reminders, and directions for you as you move through the rest of the handbook. Pay close attention, underline things, reread parts, treat this book as if your life depends on it. Although it *may* be an exaggeration to say your life depends on it, it's *not* an exaggeration to say your happiness does.

6

Supporting Yourself and Your Partner

This chapter is about educating you on how to support your partner in becoming aware of subconscious patterns of behavior he or she might have developed in dealing with (or perhaps better, not dealing with) his or her grief. You will soon see that this support is also a part of your own commitment to TOTAL HONESTY. Let's look at a typical example of acting on a subconscious and incomplete behavior pattern resulting from grief.

SHORT-TERM RELIEF DOESN'T WORK

Two years after John's younger brother died, he was visiting his other brother. He'd gone to his brother's office and was waiting for him to finish a business meeting. As he waited, he glanced into the office next door and was stunned by what he saw. He quickly found his brother and asked him who the boy was in the other office. His brother said that the boy worked for him. He wasn't sure why he hired him—the boy really wasn't qualified. John then led his brother down to the other office and had him stand in the doorway. He took a picture of their younger brother out of his wallet and held it up where they could compare the picture and the features of the boy who worked for him. The young man looked like a twin of their brother. Having him in the workplace illustrates the need that John's older brother had to act on a subconscious and incomplete grieving pattern. This is "Short-Term Relief."

Another example of this pattern is demonstrated in our society by the behavior of grievers at cemeteries. It's not uncommon for people to visit grave sites on an extremely regular basis for years following the death. People feel as if the death robbed them of the chance to complete their business, and so they will often visit the place that best helps them feel close to their loved one. Unconsciously, the griever is seeking some relief from the pain caused by the incomplete relationship. The problem is that these visits don't lead to any permanent relief or completion with the person who died. This was explained in the section on enshrinement in Chapter 2.

Short-term relief has no lasting effect, and can in fact become a separate issue unto itself. Huge numbers of grievers, looking for some relief from their pain, are given medication. Medication will absolutely give short-term relief. But if the griever takes the pills for too long, drug addiction may become the problem. Many people take a drink to relieve their agony. Here again, if no real solution is found, the agony continues and the drinking continues. The next thing you know, there is an alcohol problem. Some people overeat, others isolate themselves by becoming overly involved in work or hobbies. Short-term feeling relief is like being a hamster on a wheel—no matter how fast you go, you make no progress.

Over a long period of time the griever begins to feel

hopeless. It's as if the pain will never end. After a while even the most supportive friends and family tire of the bereaved's grief, and then the isolation, aloneness, and "ACADEMY AWARD" Recovery follow.

You are now becoming the most supportive friend your partner has. Since both of you have read and understood who is responsible for your attitudes, feelings, and actions regarding the loss, it is important that you begin to support one another in being aware of when you participate in this isolation, aloneness, or "ACADEMY AWARD" Recovery. It is important that you begin to support one another in not acting on subconscious short-term relief. In trying to deal with the pain, despair, and loneliness caused by loss, we've always been surrounded by well-meaning friends who have always tried to make it easier for us.

The approach never works. Our friends have allowed us to act on these subconscious patterns, which makes it easier for us now, but never better for us later. We call this the "easier now" theory. There is no easy way to process loss. This handbook and its step-by-step program is a simple way, but it's not easy. It's not designed to make it easier for you; it is designed to make it *better* for you. If there were an easy way to do what must be done, we'd tell you. What we can tell you is that if you're willing to do this work, you can recover.

Do not let the relationship you are forming with your partner become one of making it easy for each other to feel complete with this work. Be thorough with yourselves and each other. Every time you feel complete with the exercise you're on, the meeting you're in, or the chapter you're reading, check out this feeling of being complete with your partner before moving on. Tell your partner to be totally honest with you on how thorough you're being in doing this work. The "easier now" theory is never better in the long run.

After John's infant son died, a doctor prescribed medication. He was trying to make it easier for John. He didn't know that protecting John from his pain would only make his grief more difficult:

> "Friends didn't want to talk about the death. They made the topic of my son's death off-limits. Years later, I asked them why. They said, 'Talking about the death would rekindle old pain.'
>
> "They didn't want to see me hurt any more. They thought they were loving me.
>
> "None of these well-meaning people knew that by trying to make it easier for me, they were making my grief more intense. They thought that they were loving me, but in fact they almost loved me to death.
>
> "I kept all that pain inside until I was ready to explode. It was very much like being a time bomb.
>
> "Somehow, I knew that talking about my feelings would be good for me, even though it frightened me. But everyone around kept acting like it wasn't appropriate to talk about my painful feelings. With enough messages of this nature, I soon began to question my own sanity. I decided something was wrong with me. I couldn't see any end to the pain. I began to entertain the idea of ending it all."

The sad part of all this is that a large number of grievers do indeed commit suicide. This is truly a national disgrace.

Many others elect not to live. Even though they still walk, talk, and breathe, there is no real life left in them. Since no one wants to talk about grief, grievers don't know that their thoughts are in fact normal. They then feel isolated and alone, as if no one understands.

We all know that the death of a loved one is life's most painful event. You also need to know that the pain must be confronted directly. This will make it better, as opposed to easier.

So, for the sake of your own and your partner's aliveness, tell the truth when you feel that either of you is isolating with subconscious short-term relief. The choice is between increasing your participation by doing this work, or continuing to contribute to each other's isolation by making it "easier now" instead of better in the long run.

DENYING THE TRUTH DOESN'T WORK

Here is another concept that is important for you to understand while working with your partner. We've all heard statements that grievers practice denial. This is most often said about the death itself:

"She's in denial about the death."

"He has to accept that she's dead."

Although denial is in fact a part of grief, it is seldom denial about the fact that a death occurred. In almost all cases, one of the first calls made after a death is to the local funeral home. Grievers always make clear statements that prove they're not denying the death itself:

"My dad has died."

"Mother has passed away."

"He expired."

"Her pain is over now."

Doesn't sound like anyone is denying the death, does it? And yet we said that denial is part of grief. So, if it's not the death itself that's being denied, what is it? *It is the condition of the emotional relationship that existed at the time of the death that's being denied.*

Almost immediately after the death of a loved one, grievers become aware of things about the relationship that they wish had been DIFFERENT, BETTER, OR MORE. Since the death has already occurred, they feel as if it's too late to correct these things. They feel helpless and soon try to deny that anything has been left unsaid. With all the misinformation they're carrying around about loss, as well as life, is it any wonder that their relationships are not emotionally complete?

This denying of our feelings is a result of all the early training we received about dealing with loss—another concept that is sometimes difficult for partners in this work to be aware of on their own. Through your partner's support you can begin to be aware of when you are participating in denial of your feelings. This is part of the beginning of your recovery process.

STEP FIVE: RECOGNIZING SHORT-TERM RELIEF AND DENIAL

So far, all the steps in this program have been designed to give the alliance between you and your partner a firm foundation. All the steps after this one will center more on your recovery and less on your partnership. There are sixteen steps in this program for moving beyond loss. These steps will guide you through five stages of recovery. We have known grief recovery partners to move through these steps thoroughly in a two-week period. Most have taken a month. If after two months you and your partner have not arrived at the last step, we suggest you start over or find a new partner. The best way to prevent this from happening is with this step of supporting one another in recognizing short-term relief and denial.

Following his father's death, Frank gained thirty pounds within the next three months. He gained twenty more three months later. At a recommended body weight of one hundred and fifty pounds, this qualified him for obesity. He was supported in this behavior by late-night denial of his feelings, which led him to the short-term feeling relief of obsessively consuming chocolate cookies, ice cream, and milk. This is a classic example of short-term relief resulting from a denial of feelings.

What short-term feeling relief are you using? There have been several examples given in this chapter. Read the chapter out loud with your partner in your next meeting. Then have a discussion about what you read.

During your discussion, tell your partner about at least two examples of short-term relief you have used to deny your feelings since the loss. This step is not as easy as it appears. It could be your first chance to demonstrate your commitment to total honesty. At the end of the meeting make an agreement with your partner to inform one another each time you are aware of reacting to denial by participating in short-term feeling relief.

The next chapter is about an exercise that will assist you in uncovering these patterns for yourself and your partner so the two of you can begin to acquire a new awareness of how not to act on them.

7

The Loss History Graph

Once a habit of doing anything is established, we continue to use the habit unconsciously. Our lives are made up of many habits. You've probably been putting on the same shoe first all your life and never thought about it until right now. This is also probably true of how you've been trying to deal with the losses in your life. That's why a Loss History Graph is so important. We need to know what our pattern is so we can confront and change it. And we need to break our isolation.

The primary purpose of this chapter is to create a detailed examination of the loss events in your life and to identify the patterns that have resulted from them (along the lines we saw for John in Chapter 2). Its secondary purpose is to help ensure a feeling of unity or closeness between you and your partner.

We're all going to have other losses during our lives and we don't want to fall into the same old traps. As the old mountain man told the young mountain man, "If you want to avoid bear traps, it's a good idea to know what they look like."

What We Learned About Loss

In order to do a Loss History Graph, it's a good idea to know what it looks like. Here are ours:

JOHN W. JAMES

BORN: *February 16, 1944*

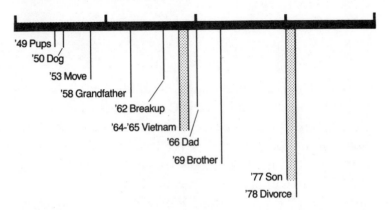

'49 Pups
'50 Dog
'53 Move
'58 Grandfather
'62 Breakup
'64-'65 Vietnam
'66 Dad
'69 Brother
'77 Son
'78 Divorce

'49 Puppies—As a starting point, I'll tell you about my earliest conscious memory. My first memory is from the day our family dog gave birth to a litter of puppies. I must have noticed our dog looking or acting strange for several weeks prior to that night and may have even asked about it but I don't remember it.

I vaguely remember my father mentioning that tonight would probably be the night because our dog kept dragging scraps of paper and old towels to her bed. I don't think I even knew what he was talking about when he made that comment. Late that night, after my brother and I had gone to sleep, our father woke us up. He took us to the dog's bed. Our dog, who had always been friendly, seemed to be suspicious and wary. I remember being a little frightened. As my dad brought us closer to the bed, I could see three or four little lumps near her. Soon she began to whine and move around. I thought that she was in pain and wanted to help her. My father told us to stay back, that she was having trouble delivering one of the puppies. When he said that, it dawned on me what the little lumps were. I was happy, scared, proud, and confused all at the same time. Eventually my father had to help her give birth to the last three puppies.

My brother and I wanted to hold and pet the puppies right away but we were told that our dog might not like that, so we went back to bed. Of course we couldn't sleep and spent half the night talking about this wondrous event. The next two weeks were spent being solicitous of our dog and waiting for the puppies to open their eyes.

This event is the very first conscious memory that I've been able to identify. I have no earlier recollection of anything.

'50 Dog—This is the year my dog died. (That loss was discussed in Chapter 2.)

'53 Punishment—When I was unjustly punished and lost my trust in adults at some level.

'53 Moving—When we moved for the first time. Moving is a major loss for children. My parents

explained all the intellectual reasons why we were moving: it was a better neighborhood, a better house, it was closer to school, and we would own it rather than rent. That didn't make it feel any better. I was going to miss my friends.

'58 Grandfather—When my grandfather died.

'62 Girlfriend—When my girlfriend and I broke up.

'64/65 Vietnam—In all honesty, my Vietnam War experience is the one remaining unresolved grief issue in my life. I have been working on aspects of this loss almost continually for the past two years.

The way Vietnam veterans were treated in our society reinforced the loss of trust experience. It is this loss of trust that causes so many problems for veterans even to this day. As a society, we have paid and are still paying dearly for this. During the years of the war we suffered the deaths of more than 58,000 combat troops; in the years since the war ended we have felt the loss by suicide of more than three times that number.

'66 Father—This is the year my father died. I had only seen him once since I came home from overseas; much was unfinished in our relationship. His drinking had continued until it finally killed him. It was a very painful experience for me.

'69 Brother—My younger brother, a twenty-year-old pole vaulter at Southern Illinois University, was in perfect health when he died. He

was on his way to visit me in southern California where I lived at the time. He was traveling with two of his friends from college; they'd stopped for the night and had all decided to take a nap. Later that afternoon when his friends went to waken him, they found that he had died.

I spent days trying to find some intellectual reason for his death, and when I couldn't find one, I assigned blame for his death to God.

'77 Son—This is the year my son died. Two years earlier, my wife and I had had a daughter. Her arrival was the high point of my life. When my wife became pregnant again, I was looking forward to another such experience. About five months into the pregnancy, complications set in. When my wife went into premature labor, we raced to the hospital where every possible medical technique was employed to slow or stop the process. She was hooked up to monitoring devices and for two days we had to listen to a perfectly healthy heartbeat while knowing there was little chance the child would live.

All of my life I had been taught to believe certain things about what my job was as a man, a husband, and a father. I had been taught to believe that it was my job to identify problems and solve them. What I discovered right away was that it did not matter who I knew, what I knew, how much money I had, or how intelligent I was—there was nothing I could do. It was the most frustrating experience I had ever had.

Despite all the medical intervention, our son was born. For the first eight hours, it appeared that everything would be all right. Then things started to go wrong. Once again, identifying the problem was easy. I could see the problem: he was about 2 pounds, had black hair, and was encased in a glass box. But there was nothing I could do but stand and look at all the monitoring equipment and feel impotent.

This went on for two days. I was trying to help my wife because that was what I had been taught to do. There is nothing wrong with that except, in trying to help her, I was not acknowledging my own pain. At the end of the second day, my son just breathed out and never breathed in again.

If you can believe this, it started to go downhill from there. The things people said and did were shocking. The inability of my wife and me to talk became apparent. Our relationship began to fall apart immediately. During the next eight months, I went everywhere, talked to everyone, and read everything that I could get my hands on to help ease the pain. This was the point where I discovered there was little or no help available to deal with the grief. That was real despair.

'78 Divorce—This is the year my wife and I were divorced. The divorce happened because we had no idea how to deal with the grief caused by all the changes in our lives. We were newly married, new

parents, and new grievers at the same time. The death of our son was the straw that broke the camel's back.

In typical griever fashion, my mind was preoccupied with thoughts of things that I wished I had done in a way that was DIFFERENT, BETTER, or MORE. If I hadn't made the cost of medical bills such an issue, my wife might have gone for medical checkups more frequently. The night the emergency started, we had no baby sitter and had no real idea of the seriousness of my wife's condition, so I didn't go with her to the doctor's office. I used to sit and think about how frightening that must have been for her. Even as all of these thoughts were running through my mind, I had no skill or practice at being able to talk about what I was feeling. I felt isolated and alone, yet truly believed that I was supposed to be strong and keep it all inside. Since that was all I knew, that is what I did. With that type of pressure building up, arguments became common. Hurt feelings were then added to the fire and more arguments followed. At the same time my wife was thinking that if she hadn't gotten pregnant so soon after the birth of our daughter, then none of this would have happened. That was her DIFFERENT, BETTER, OR MORE type of thinking. She, too, had no knowledge about the importance of talking about her feelings.

When communication breaks down in a marriage, no matter the cause, it is only a matter of time before divorce occurs. When the divorce takes place, we have yet another grieving experience to deal with, so the cycle continues.

While writing this book, I called my former wife to discuss her thoughts about telling this part of the story. One of the things she shared with me was how she had not known for several years how much the death of our son had affected me. How could she have possibly known? I was an "ACADEMY AWARD" griever then.

FRANK CHERRY

BORN: *June 21, 1953*

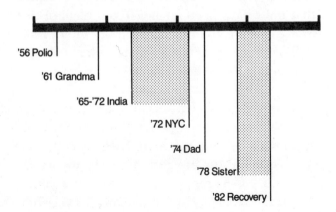

'56 Polio
'61 Grandma
'65-'72 India
'72 NYC
'74 Dad
'78 Sister
'82 Recovery

'56 Polio—My earliest memory is of when I was three years old and my father had taken me to the doctor for a polio shot. I can remember this cold, hard, green vinyl table the nurse placed me on, and I saw the needle they were going to use. The nurse had these big white-soled shoes (remember, I was only three) and her whole appearance scared me

terribly. It terrified me so much that I couldn't even accept the candy she offered when it was all over. She had to give it to my father to take home.

Most of what I remember about my childhood are fond and happy events, so this one would definitely qualify as a grieving experience. We were living in Seattle that summer, which was a long way from our home in Texas. My sister, who was five years older than me, was my only friend. She was bigger than me, stronger than me, and ran a lot faster. All the children I remember in that neighborhood were her age. During this time I definitely felt "less than" all that was around me. This whole experience affected my ability to trust and began to convince me that the world was a hostile place.

'61 Grandma—The next significant loss came when my grandmother died. She was my father's mother, and it was my first real conscious experience with death. Even though I was not that close to her, there was grief and fear surrounding the entire event. The most devastating thing to me was how much it distressed my father. At this point in my childhood he had become a hero for me. It terrified me to know that anything in life could upset my hero so much. It reaffirmed my earlier belief that the world is a hostile place. I had lost my hero, who had told me that I'd better get a good education, that it was the one thing no one could ever take from me.

At this time there was a good friend of mine,

this kid that lived behind our house in Texas. He used to make plastic model airplanes and let me play with them. When I started making model airplanes, he wanted to play with mine. I told him if he touched one, I'd burn his house down. This was after my grandmother's death. I was so afraid that things would be taken from me. It was as though my volume knob was turned up, my time bomb ticked. Yet at this time of my life I could only operate with the attitude "I'd better get mine before you take it away from me."

'65–'72 India/New York—This time in my life was a grieving experience caused by the loss of familiar surroundings and familiar behavior. My father took my family on a business trip to Chandagar, India. We spent three months there while he taught their university professors about electronics. I was twelve years old and this was a strange and hostile environment for me—and a long way from Texas. During this period I began my teenage years. Wanting to be an adult, not wanting to be an adult, wanting acceptance, experiencing the pressures of dating, being torn between family values and peer pressure, were all contributing factors in my detachment. This culminated in my leaving all that was familiar and isolating myself with my studies in New York City at the age of nineteen.

As I discussed earlier, this led to a lifestyle that no one in my family could know about or would approve of. Not that there weren't happy times during these seven years; it's just that in looking back, I realized there was an underlying incomplete grief to this part of my life. It was during this period that I was finally convinced that love is scarce. It would be ten long years before I realized that this was an erroneous belief.

'74 Dad—As you can see, this is the second longest line on my graph. The sudden nature of my father's death and the condition of our relationship when he died made this an extremely painful experience for me. It shocked me into the reality of how dangerous my use of narcotics was at this time. For the next four years I read every self-help book I could find; became analyzed, actualized, realized, meditationized; recommitted myself to the studies of communications; and did all I could at the time to correct the problems that had developed between me and my family.

All of this led me to a very close relationship with my sister and her family. By this time she was married and had a son. This period also reaffirmed my belief that if I didn't protect all that I had, the world would try to take it away from me—an extension of my earlier belief that the world was a hostile place.

'78 Sister—This is the beginning of the worst period of grief in my life. Given my family's background, my sister turned out to be the scholar that everyone expected. She had a Ph.D. and was

teaching philosophy at the University of Köln in Germany when she became ill with a Type C hepatitis—a very severe form of the disease that landed her in the hospital immediately. For nine months she tried to fight back. During one episode she burst a blood vessel in her brain and became completely dependent on life-support systems to keep her alive. She fell in and out of two comas. Her husband, son, mother, and brother watched as the decision was made to take her off the life supports and let her die.

At this point in my life, I was convinced that if there was a God, I wanted very little to do with Him. The next four years were some of the most financially rewarding for me, which aggravated my isolation. This isolation led me to the most emotional and spiritual demoralization of my life: it led me to the depths of alcoholism.

'82 Recovery—The lowest point on my graph. This was my greatest grief, for two reasons. The first is that this was the end result of all my previous incomplete loss experiences. The second is that all the medication (drugs and alcohol) had stopped working for me. I had been using these things to deal with loss since my teenage years. Through friends with similar experiences I knew where to go for recovery, but I did not believe it would work for me. When this loss occurred, I was convinced that there was no hope.

It *did* work, and at the time of this writing has been maintained for over five years.

In Chapter 2, we were able to identify six things that John came to believe were true as a result of early loss experiences. Those six things are:

1. Bury your feelings
2. Replace the loss
3. Grieve alone
4. Just give it time
5. Regret the past (DIFFERENT, BETTER, OR MORE)
6. Don't trust

Just as John had to survey his own life, so you too must begin to discover what specific beliefs you learned about how to deal with loss. These beliefs, however misguided, must be identified between you and your partner in light of total honesty. These misguided beliefs are what lead us into denial of our feelings and short-term relief.

WILL YOU THINK ABOUT, TALK ABOUT, OR TAKE RECOVERY ACTION?

Where grief recovery is concerned, there are three categories of people—those who:

1. THINK about taking recovery action
2. TALK about taking recovery action
3. TAKE recovery action

The decision you must make is to ask yourself honestly which category you're in and then—which is most often necessary—shift to the third category which will allow you to recover. Sounds simple, doesn't it? Well, it is.

These categories are demonstrated around us all the time and are shown in all walks of life. Many people THINK about making changes in their lives; ten years later, they're still thinking about it. We've all encountered the ones who TALK about doing something different in their lives; the next time we see them, they're still talking about it. The people we admire are the ones who go through the categories in order and then achieve the desired result. These are the ones who TAKE the action.

Some years ago, a man had an idea about doing something to make the world a better place. He THOUGHT about what had to be done for some time—it was going to be a monumental job. For the next few months he TALKED with others about his idea, and some of them told him how difficult or perhaps impossible it might turn out to be. Finally, he began to TAKE action.

Each Labor Day we get to see the result on television. We get to see the result of someone going through the steps in their proper order to arrive at the goal. The man's name is Jerry Lewis.

Jerry Lewis THOUGHT about doing something about muscular dystrophy. He TALKED to some other people about it. We all know and can see each year the result of his ACTION.

Now it's your turn. Are you going to THINK about taking recovery action, TALK about taking recovery action, or are you going to TAKE recovery action?

It takes courage, commitment, and effort to do this seemingly simple step. We also know that if you're this far along in the book, you have what it takes to continue.

STEP SIX: PREPARING YOUR LOSS HISTORY GRAPH

Grief is the thing that robs you of your happiness. We want you to face it, resolve it, and be better prepared to help not only yourself but others as well. In order to be successful, you need to know as much about your personal patterns as possible. You need to uncover all the significant emotional loss experiences you've ever had in order to discover the early childhood patterns you were influenced in forming. Those are likely the very patterns you're using today to deal with the current loss. Some of your patterns may be the same as ours ("Replace the loss," "Grieve alone") and some may be different. The best place to begin is at the beginning.

We'll give the instructions for the Loss History Graph exercise just as we do in our seminars:

1. We strongly suggest that you start this exercise no more than twenty-four hours before your next scheduled meeting with your partner. The entire exercise should not take you more than an hour, so if possible start it just before your next meeting is to begin. We have found that strong feelings are often stirred while partners prepare this exercise. More productive meetings result when the partners bring to them such intense emotions, which have not had a chance to dissipate over a longer time interval.

When you have an emotional reaction, let it be okay with you. You're finally experiencing the feelings you've been hiding for so long. If you get an emotional response to losses, ask yourself, what does it feel like?

Do you still miss them? What were you told at the time of the loss?

We also want to caution you about anger that could occur as the result of doing the Loss History Graph. It may be anger directed at those who influenced you concerning grief. It may be anger at yourself when you see how many feelings you've avoided over the years. There is nothing wrong with anger if you share it with your partner and let it go. Sharing your true feelings is how you defuse the time bomb.

2. The writing part of the exercise is nonverbal. It is best done alone and in silence. Find a place and time that will provide you with these surroundings. It will help your concentration.

3. Get a pen or pencil and a piece of blank paper, at least the size of typing paper or standard notebook paper (8½" by 11"); legal-size paper (8½" by 14") is even better. Place the paper horizontally on your desk or table. Write your name and birthdate at the top of the paper. (For some of you, this is your first chance to put total honesty to the test. Put down the *real* year you were born.)

4. Draw a straight line across the center of the page. Then divide your line into four equal parts,

marking the sections lightly with a pencil. This will give you a reference for where to plot dates, like this:

So, if you are eighty years old, at the halfway point you were forty; if you are fifty years old, at the halfway point you were twenty-five; if you are twenty-six years old, at the halfway point you were thirteen; and so on. (If you're getting frustrated with our detailed instructions here, just remember that this is where most people get confused and stop doing the work. We feel we can't emphasize this enough.) Write the current date on the right end of the line. Then plot your "dawn of memory," or earliest recollection, whether you perceive it as a loss or not.

Both of our examples began with our earliest conscious memory. If you think hard, you'll find that your first recollection will fall between ages two and five. It need not be good or bad, happy or sad; it is just an event or experience. This can be called the beginning or "dawn of memory." Some people can remember further back; if you can, that's okay. If you can't find something before age five, consider that there may be an early loss so painful you've blocked it out. This is not an unusual response to childhood pain. If you think this is true, see if a phone call can be made to a relative or friend and ask if anything happened. Put some effort into this. Later it will prove to be important in the discussion you'll have with your partner.

5. Now set a timer or alarm clock for one hour from the time you start and mark your losses on the line. You don't have to spend too much time writing out at length each separate grieving experience as we did in our examples. Just make simple notes of words

or phrases that will remind you of the loss when it's time to discuss it with your partner.

6. You might be thinking, "Mark my losses on the line? Where do I begin?"

Earlier, in our discussion of TOTAL HONESTY, we mentioned skeletons in the closet. If there is anything that you have ever done that you've never told anyone about, see if you're willing to start there. If not, plot the most significant loss first. As in Frank's example, this could be a series of losses over a period of time. This will give you the "low" point on your graph, and you can work up from there.

Try not to let the timer or being too accurate pressure you. On the other hand, be thorough. If you find that a half hour has gone by and all you have plotted is your "dawn of memory" and one other loss, then mark whatever it is you're thinking of at the moment. Remember, it's not just death we have to plot here. Losses include moving, changing schools, changing jobs, outgrowing a friend, divorce, etc. Just keep going. Your thoughts will start to flow. Our experience has shown us that most people over the age of fourteen will have at least five losses to plot. Don't worry, you'll find that an hour is plenty of time.

7. It is necessary for you to understand the vertical lines on our examples. The length of the lines refers to the intensity of that loss event. The farther the line goes down the paper, the more traumatic the experience was.

8. Don't try to get this "right." Get it honest. There are no grades given for this work, no one's approval is

acquired. Abandon yourself to the exercise and you will receive benefit directly proportional to the amount you put into it. Impress yourself with how honest and thorough you can be.

9. You're on your own . . . begin!

STEP SEVEN: SHARING YOUR LOSS HISTORY GRAPH

Congratulations on finishing your graph!

Now go see your partner. Be sure you choose a place where you can be alone and undisturbed together. Remember and recommit yourself to TOTAL HONESTY and ABSOLUTE CONFIDENTIALITY. Before you begin, read these instructions out loud with your partner.

First, share your thoughts about your earliest conscious memory. The story about your "dawn of memory" will tell your partner much about your childhood and the surroundings you came from. You need to share with each other the story of your youth and what you were taught to believe. Don't be afraid. You're going to find out that you both have a lot of the same misinformation.

After talking about your "dawn of memory," start at the first loss and discuss the feelings you had at the time. Continue along the graph and help your partner understand how you were feeling as each event took place. Begin to defuse the time bomb. Let your feelings be okay. Some of the losses on your graph will be more painful to discuss than others.

When you finish sharing your graph, be sure you and

your partner agree on what the *one* most painful loss was for you to discuss. If you find that more than one loss was equally painful to talk about, then choose the most recent. We want you to choose and determine one loss for you to work with for the rest of the book. We will expand on what to do with other losses at the beginning of the next chapter. For now, just be concerned with the one you agree on.

We would also like you and your partner to determine what you were influenced to believe. The beliefs could be similar to ours or perhaps you'll find new and different ones. They can include:

- Bury your feelings
- Replace the loss
- Grieve alone
- Just give it time
- Regret the past (DIFFERENT, BETTER, OR MORE)
- Don't trust
- Be seen and not heard
- Protect yourself
- Don't get involved, they'll only leave you anyway
- Get all you can before it's taken away from you
- Don't expect anything

Write yours down as you go along or have your partner write them down for you. When you are done, look to see if there was a pattern confirming your beliefs. Look to see if you found a pattern in your reaction to each loss. At the end of sharing your graph it's your partner's turn. Simply reverse your roles. At that time you might find it helpful to review these instructions.

Now, it's time for one of you to begin. Don't THINK about it or TALK about it. Just TAKE action, and one of you start! Don't put the burden of going first on your partner— you go first. A typical start could sound like this: "I've done my graph and I'm really angry with myself. I see now how many feelings I've been hiding for years. My earliest conscious memory was . . ."

Begin sharing your graphs here. When both you and your partner are done, continue your reading.

Often people report to us that a newly found feeling of union and closeness with their partner develops at this point. It's also not uncommon for people to realize that their partner now knows as much or more about them as some of their own family members.

Through the Loss History Graph we get to see how much alike we are as grievers and human beings. Yet we are still individuals. Scientists tell us that nowhere on the planet are there any two snowflakes, crystals, grains of sand, leaves, or atoms alike. None of them behaves quite the same way. Yet they're all made of the same ingredients. With this exercise we can simultaneously see our similarities and our differences. This realization can truly be a moving experience for you and your partner. Through participation and communication it doesn't take long to create a feeling of intimacy.

As have many participants in our seminars, you may be inspired to go out, have dinner, and enjoy the new relationship you've created with your partner. Yet before

you do this, we ask that the session not conclude until you
have discovered:

1. The one loss for you and the one loss for your partner to work on for the rest of the book,

2. A list of beliefs you acquired from experiencing
   grief, and

3. A date, time, and location for the next meeting with
   your partner. (Give yourselves at least the night off
   to read through Step 8 in the next chapter.)

PART THREE

Finding the Solution

Welcome to the third part of this handbook, "Finding the Solution." As stated in Chapter 1, the solution is made up of five stages you must move through in order to recover from a grieving experience. These stages and their meanings are:

1. Gaining Awareness—that an incomplete emotional relationship exists.
2. Accepting Responsibility—that in part you are the cause of its existence.
3. Identifying Recovery Communications—that you have not delivered.
4. Taking Actions—to communicate them.
5. Moving Beyond Loss—through sharing with others.

Separate chapters will explain and guide you through each stage of this program. You'll have to be aware of the things you've read earlier, so treat this book as you would a textbook. Mark it up, underline the important parts, outline portions if that's how you study. Each chapter will include actions and small steps that will lead you toward recovery. As we explained earlier, these steps will also require your open-mindedness and much willingness and courage.

Keep in mind, this is your life and your happiness we're working on. We're sure that just reading along so far and doing the exercises has reminded you and your partner of some painful experiences. You've probably already negotiated with yourself several times about whether to keep going. If you have done the work described to this point, you and your partner have shown incredible willingness to recover. You deserve a hug and a pat on the back. So be sure to acknowledge yourself and your partner for getting this far. The choice to recover is always yours, and requires a recommitment to each small step along the way.

8

Gaining Awareness

You're probably more aware now of grief and reaction to loss than you've ever been in your life. How you became ill-prepared to deal with grief is probably much clearer to you now. How those around you were ill-equipped to be of any real assistance to you is also probably much clearer to you. You've worked on and identified what you were influenced to believe in your Loss History Graph. You have also identified one loss to work on for the rest of the book.

We have one more step to take before working specifically on the loss you've chosen. That step is to identify all losses you are still emotionally incomplete with. This knowledge will be important to your progression through this first stage of your recovery. As you move through the stage of gaining awareness, your perspective on other incomplete losses will change. To be conscious of this change, it is important that we identify these losses first.

AWARENESS OF EMOTIONALLY INCOMPLETE LOSSES

In essence, your Loss History Graph was an inventory on past grieving experiences. Only after taking such an inventory and discussing it with your partner will the two of you be able to identify which loss or losses are still causing you grief. These are the losses that are emotionally incomplete.

When you're reminded of any loss from the past, if your first response is one of pain or discomfort in thinking of it or discussing it, then you are emotionally incomplete with it. This means the reminder negatively affects your happiness. On the other hand, if you felt safe and secure while meeting with your partner and a reminder of a loss from the past did not affect your emotional state, then it is not still causing you pain and you are complete with it. It's no longer affecting your happiness.

We have feelings in response to every life change that occurs. The more intense these feelings are, the closer they come to grief. Most of these changes are small and insignificant and have caused you little or no discomfort during your life. Yet some have had a lasting effect on your attitude and outlook on life. This effect has resulted in the list of beliefs you and your partner made while sharing your Loss History Graph. Most of the people who attend our seminars find they have two or three unresolved issues to deal with. Their original motivation comes from a recent loss, but as they get involved with the steps, they discover other unresolved or incomplete losses.

For your perspective to be somewhat limited by emotional involvement is quite normal. This is because you're the griever. This is why it's impossible to recover alone. You'll need the objective opinion of your partner to help you identify those losses that were difficult for you to communicate about.

STEP EIGHT: IDENTIFYING EMOTIONALLY INCOMPLETE LOSSES

At the next meeting you have with your partner you will be doing this step of identifying emotionally incomplete losses. In this step you will review your Loss History Graphs and pick the losses that are still painful for you. Here are some questions that will help you and your partner determine which losses you are still emotionally incomplete with:

- Which ones caused your throat to get tight when you shared them?

- Which ones elicited an emotional response when you were sharing them with your partner?

- If you cried while sharing your Loss History Graph, when did the crying begin? At what point in your story?

- If you didn't cry, did you feel sad? When did the sadness begin?

- Did you cry while your partner shared? You may have been reminded of another loss that you have been burying for a long time. If you haven't already shared this with your partner, this exercise is the time to disclose it.

Here are your instructions for this step:

1. Bring your Loss History Graph to the next meeting with your partner. Talk about what's happened and how you've felt since sharing it—if you've felt better, if you've felt worse, if your reactions have been

more positive, if they've been more negative or haven't changed at all since sharing the graph, any of these responses are okay. There is no part of this step-by-step program you can get right. You can only get it honest. The only assessment that can be made of how you and your partner are doing is through thoroughness, honesty, and confidentiality. So, during this discussion evaluate how each of you is doing in these three areas. Be thorough, be honest, be gentle, and remember you love one another.

2. Read out loud everything in the introduction to Part Three and everything in this exercise of the handbook. Alternate your reading: you read two paragraphs, your partner reads two paragraphs. At the end of each turn, stop and discuss anything you relate to, anything you don't relate to, or anything that you didn't hear or understand.

3. When you are done with your reading, get out your Loss History Graphs. One of you go first and consult with your partner in making a list of all the losses you feel you're still incomplete with. Be honest in your assessment. If your partner does not agree with your list, your partner is probably right. Therefore, if you don't think you're incomplete with a specific loss on your graph and your partner does think you're incomplete with it, put the loss on your list. It doesn't matter how many or how long ago the loss happened. If you still do not know whether you're incomplete regarding any loss on your graph, simply ask your partner. Your partner will probably have a

better perspective on which losses were especially difficult for you to talk about than you do. It's like the catcher in a baseball game sometimes having a better image of the whole situation than the pitcher does. His perspective is different. It's much like the saying, "We can't see the forest for the trees."

4. After making your list, once again schedule the date, time, and location of your next meeting. Give yourselves at least the night off to read the next section on your own and make a Relationship Graph. If you aren't doing so already, at this point in the exercises we suggest ending each meeting with a hug. (If there are more than two of you, make it a group hug.)

AWARENESS OF YOUR INCOMPLETE RELATIONSHIP

In order to resolve an emotionally incomplete loss, we must complete it. If you complete your emotional relationship, *it does not mean you'll have to forget your loved one.* The only thing to keep you from going on is fearing that you'll forget your loved one. That is not going to happen. What we're talking about is completing your emotional relationship with the list of beliefs you've made, rather than with your loved one. The pain, isolation, and loneliness that results from these beliefs cuts you off from forgotten memories and a new life.

Acquiring any common behavioral skill makes a wonderful analogy for what we're talking about. Let's assume most readers have learned to ride a bicycle. Let's also assume that most readers remember learning how to ride a bicycle. During this learning process you probably fell off the bike a few times. This was a painful reminder that you had not yet mastered the skill. Therefore, any reminder of bicycles at this point in your learning process could lead to a reminder of the pain. You were still open to the effect of these reminders because you had not yet acquired the skill. But knowing that others had learned this skill motivated you to keep trying, so you climbed back on the bike, and this time you went a little farther.

Let's say that this time you were doing much better and decided to go off the sidewalk and onto the street. But you had to jump the curb and that didn't work. You fell again and it was even more painful. Your lack of ability to ride a bicycle was definitely affecting your choices. Finally, when you reached the point of acquiring this skill, you had a greater freedom of choice.

You've never forgotten how to ride a bike and you've probably never forgotten that there was pain in learning to ride a bike. Yet, any reminder of your relationship with bicycles is no longer painful. You completed your relationship with the pain of learning to ride through acquiring the skill. So, recovery from grief doesn't mean forgetting the event or the relationship. It means completing your relationship with the pain of the event by acquiring the skill to move through the steps of recovery.

We begin by completing a Relationship Graph in

order to find out what it is about the loss that's emotionally incomplete. There are many reasons for doing this graph, not the least of which is our poor memory. We know that memory is enormously fallible. Our poor memory is also affected by being emotionally incomplete with the deceased.

When death occurs, if we're trapped into wishing things could have been DIFFERENT, BETTER, OR MORE, we become critical. We either become critical of what we did or did not do, or we become critical of what they did or did not do. During this critical phase we tend to build inaccurate memories of our relationship with the deceased. The more we participate in building these inaccurate memories, the more difficult it is to complete our grief.

WHAT WE DID OR DID NOT DO IN OUR RELATIONSHIP If we become critical of what we did or did not do, it usually leads to an inaccurate appraisal of ourselves and an inaccurate appraisal of our loved one. The appraisal of ourselves becomes too critical and more often than not the appraisal of our loved one is too complimentary. We've talked to grievers following the death of a loved one and in no time at all they began telling us about someone who never made a mistake his or her entire life. It's as if they're talking only about the good and positive aspects of their loved one's life. When we listen closely, we'll even hear their guilt: "I should have appreciated him more while I had him. He was a perfect husband."

Why would any woman want to complete an emotional relationship with the perfect husband? We're sure he was the perfect husband for her, and men like that are not a dime a dozen. Yet they are human beings, and every relationship has its ups and downs that both parties are responsible for. If we're remembering our loved ones as we wished they were, not as they truly were, it is impossible to complete our emotional relationship with them. An accurate memory of our loved ones is much stronger and will be cherished more than a fantasy about them.

We recently overheard a grandfather telling his second grandson:

"Tommy was a perfect child."

We heard the grandfather begin to berate himself for not spending more time with his first grandson. We also watched the second grandson begin to deflate and isolate himself from his grandfather. In both cases the emotional incompleteness caused the grievers to feel bad about themselves and this led to an inaccurate memory of the dear child's life. The problem was caused by poor memory as well as the emotional incompleteness that existed in the relationship at the time of the death.

WHAT THEY DID OR DID NOT DO IN OUR RELATION-SHIP   If we become critical of what our loved ones did or did not do, it usually leads to an inaccurate appraisal of their entire lives and an inaccurate appraisal of our participation in the relationship. We're sure there are some people reading this book who still grieve for someone that they didn't like. Their feelings may be of strong resentment or even hate. Completing the steps up to this point in the handbook has led you to realize that you, too, are incomplete emotionally with the relationship. If what we're describing here is true for you, this program will work for you as well. We will be discussing more about resentments in relationships as we progress through the recovery stages.

THE DEATH OF A CHILD

If you are dealing with grief caused by the death of a child—including Sudden Infant Death Syndrome (SIDS), stillborn birth, miscarriage, or abortion—the beginning of your Relationship Graph will just start a bit earlier. Let's talk about when a relationship starts where a child is concerned. Generally speaking, when a woman realizes she is pregnant, her emotional relationship begins. Women also describe a change in their feelings when they feel the first "flutter" inside their body. For the next few weeks the woman is constantly saying to her husband, "Can't you feel the movement?" The husband dutifully puts his hand in the appropriate place, but can't feel movement yet. After a while, he finally feels the small kick, and that's where his emotional relationship begins.

Please understand that it's an imaginary physical relationship at this point, but it's emotionally real. When John's wife became pregnant with his son (the one who died in 1977) and he felt the first movement, his mind immediately focused on all the things he'd do

continued on next page

continued from previous page

for this child when he or she was born. His child was going to have all the things that he didn't have when he was growing up. The planning went all the way through what college he or she would attend. Although this was all a physical fantasy, it was indeed the beginning of a real emotional relationship for both John and his wife.

We often talk about completing a relationship that actually was, but in this case we need to complete a relationship that was supposed to be. When John's son died, he can remember standing outside the nursery and thinking, "He'll never know all the things I was going to do for him. He's never going to know how much I loved him."

We don't know of any parents who didn't want to give their children all the things they didn't have while growing up. Once this idea is set, what do you do with the thoughts and feelings if the child doesn't live? This type of problem needs to be completed as much as any other emotionally incomplete business.

We hope this is clear for you parents who have had a child die. For the rest of you, the graph starts with your first conscious memory or recollection of the loved one.

STEP NINE: PREPARING YOUR RELATIONSHIP GRAPH

The best way to prepare you for doing a Relationship Graph is through an example. Here's one showing John's relationship with his younger brother:

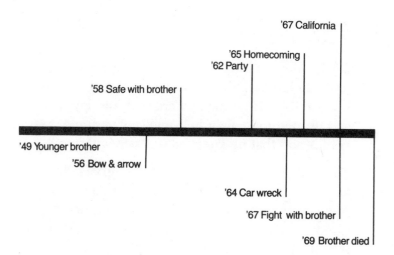

'49 is when my younger brother was born. It isn't marked above or below the line. That's because I want to tell you a story of poor communication.

I'm sure I noticed my mother was pregnant, and I must have asked her what it meant. When she told me it meant I'd have a new brother or sister, I was happy. But I must have been confused because I thought he'd be my size when he arrived. I already had an older brother so I knew brothers were my size. When they brought him home, I was shocked. He wasn't even big enough to play ball with us. That's my first conscious memory of my younger brother.

'56 is when he broke my bow and arrow. I was angry about it. I'd told him to leave it alone, but he was only seven and wanted to do all the things his

older brothers did. I was pretty rough on him and made him cry.

'58 is when he came to me for comfort and protection. Our parents had been arguing and he was terrified. He came and crawled into my bed and wanted to know if he could stay with me. I felt very proud that he knew he was safe with me.

'62 is when I went into the military service. My older brother and younger brother had a going-away party for me. They both told me they loved me and to be safe. I always knew they loved me but it was nice to hear.

'64 is when my younger brother wrecked my car. I was overseas and had told him not to use my car. Fifteen-year-olds don't listen well. So, one day when my mother was at work, he decided to go for a ride. The ride ended up at a telephone pole.

'65 is when I came home from the service. When my brother opened the front door, I couldn't believe he had grown so much. He had grown until he was bigger than I was. He'd become the man of the house. I was proud of him.

'67 was the year he lived with me in California. If you'll notice, the graph is marked both above and below the line. We had our ups and downs. He didn't want to come home when I wanted him to. I got to see what it was like to be a parent. He wouldn't make his bed. Wouldn't put gas in the car.

Ran up huge phone bills calling his girlfriend back home. At the same time we went places together, laughed, and had a great time. He and I became friends as well as brothers.

This was also the year of our biggest argument. He was talking about getting married. I didn't think that was a very good idea. We fought like cats and dogs. He eventually stayed in school and the situation calmed down. I never took the time to clear up the bad feelings.

'69 was the year my brother died. Our last conversation was over the phone. He and his friends were on their way to visit me in California. They'd stopped for the day and decided to nap. Before doing that, he called me on the phone. The boys were in Las Vegas. They'd never been there before and wanted to see the lights. As usual he was out of money and wanted to "borrow" some. I told him to go to one of the hotels where I had some friends and they'd give him some money. I hung up after saying, "See you tomorrow."

I never saw him tomorrow, he died that afternoon. How I wished, at the time, my last conversation had included, "I love you." There were other times I wished our conversations had been more feeling-oriented and honest.

John knew and loved his brother for twenty years, but when he did the Relationship Graph for the first time, not many events came to light. When he did start to remember events, at first glance they seemed to be trivial. Nevertheless, these were the things he wished he had acknowledged. It was these undelivered communications he wished had been DIFFERENT, BETTER, OR MORE.

You will be making a Relationship Graph in order to discover these communications for yourself. As with the Loss History Graph, start by drawing a line on a page. The left end is the year of your first conscious memory of your relationship with your loved one. The right end will represent the year in which the death occurred. Next, we want you to go to the beginning and reconstruct the relationship to the best of your ability. Try to recall each happy memory and each unhappy memory. Identify every misunderstanding as well as every memorable event that you possibly can. Honesty and thoroughness are essential.

The lines above horizontal are the happy or memorable experiences. Happy or above-the-line events can range anywhere from sitting together on the porch to going on vacation, holding hands as the sun sets, or raising children together.

Below horizontal are the unhappy things. Unhappy or below-the-line things can be as simple as a disagreement. Infidelity, fighting, separation, or divorce can also be below-the-line items. People do grieve over a divorced spouse who dies.

The length of the lines shows the intensity of the feelings or the significance of the event. It doesn't matter whether there are more events above or below the line; it only matters that what's on the page is the truth. Don't be concerned with what others will think or say—no one will see this but you and your partner. Remember, you've made a commitment to absolute confidentiality.

We're also not asking you to judge what happened. Why things were the way they were is not important for this particular step. Thinking about why will lead you into rationalization. Don't fall into the trap of trying to intellectualize everything. The feelings that occurred when these things happened is what we're looking for. If you must try to understand why these things happened in order to know what your feelings were at the time, then we suggest you call your partner and discuss the events with him or her. This will assist you in staying on track and keep the graph centered on this relationship. Otherwise, it can shift in focus to other surrounding relationships.

There is no real time limit on making your Relationship Graph. Our suggestion is start now and give it at least one half hour. Try to find at least five events to plot. Put it away for one full day and see if other events come to mind. If they do, add them to the graph. When you can go for one full day and not remember any more events to place on the graph, you're finished. Keep your partner posted on your daily progress. If your partner or you are still remembering events for the graph after three full days, stop where you are, schedule your next meeting, and proceed to Step 10.

STEP TEN: SHARING YOUR RELATIONSHIP GRAPH

Just as with the Loss History Graph, take this Relationship Graph to your next meeting and one of you start. A typical start could sound like this: "This thing really drove me crazy. I did the best I could with it and only came up with five things. Here they are . . . "

As you share your Relationship Graph with your partner, once again allow your feelings to be okay with you. Know you're in a safe place, be honest, and do the best you can to express how you were feeling as each event took place. Don't keep the feelings in. If you do, the only things that will result will be more isolation and more pain. You've already had enough pain. It is the suppression of feelings that makes grief take so long. All of us, at one level or another, are experts at wanting to be approved of. It is this need that causes us not to talk about feelings even when history tells us it would be good for us. The most effective way of dealing with stress and pressure is talking honestly and openly about what's going on in our lives. Not the facts and figures but the feelings. When we don't, we become the time bomb referred to earlier.

Most of the stress and pressure in life have to do with grief, yet grief is what we're least prepared to cope with. Keeping grief inside is the cause of the majority of the pain you feel. There is no reward for handling your pain alone. Quite to the contrary, there are consequences for doing that. The pain doesn't go away on its own.

When done sharing your Relationship Graph, use this checklist for making notes with your partner. Support each other in making a list of the following things:

1. How many positive or above-the-line events did you find that were never acknowledged or talked about?

2. How many negative or below-the-line events did you find that were not acknowledged, settled, or talked about?

3. Did you find other undelivered communications not covered by the above two categories?

Many times we've heard people say they wish they'd just talked more openly with their loved one. Numerous times we've heard, "I always assumed he knew I loved him. I tried to show him. I tried to show him through my actions. When he died, I realized I should have said them as well."

Once again, if you don't think something belongs on your list but your partner does, put it on. Your partner's lack of emotional involvement in your relationship with the loss will usually give the partner a better perspective. Be thorough! The following are some sample lists of the types of undelivered communications others have discovered:

Positive events other grievers did not acknowledge

> *"The first watch I got for my twelfth birthday."*
> *"Teaching me to sing."*
> *"When he learned to ride a bike."*
> *"The vacations we took to the lake."*
> *"The quiet evenings on the porch."*
> *"The week he took off from work to help me."*
> *"There were seven of us kids, but Dad always had time for me."*
> *"He always held me when I cried."*
> *"The games we played as kids."*

Negative events other grievers did not acknowledge

> *"No matter how well I did, it wasn't good enough."*

"When I was unjustly punished."

"When he drank too much."

"She always called me by my brother's name."

"When my parents divorced."

"When we moved away."

"When his lifestyle changed."

"She shut us out of her life."

"He made fun of my dreams."

"My sister teased me all the time."

"He worked so much, he was never home."

"I was sorry I acted that way."

"When my grandfather molested me."

Significant emotional statements other grievers did not deliver

"I really loved him."

"I truly appreciated the sacrifices he made."

"I was proud of her."

"I wanted to thank him."

"I was sorry that his marriage didn't work out."

"I never told her what a good mom she was."

"I'd told her I loved her many times but I feel like I got cheated out of the last opportunity to tell her one final time."

As you can see, these items all involved communications that were never acknowledged or delivered. The three categories on the checklist are the types of things incomplete relationships are made of. These are the

things that most people wish had been DIFFERENT, BET-
TER, OR MORE. These are the things causing us to want to
reach out to loved ones who have always been there, only
to find that when we need them one more time they're no
longer there.

These undelivered communications signify what
denial is all about. Since the relationship is over, it doesn't
seem as if we can ever correct these things. So we deny
that there is anything unfinished.

Undelivered communications are what you're going
to have to be willing to take partial responsibility for. Your
discovery that you could have handled some things in a
way that was DIFFERENT, BETTER, OR MORE will bring you
out of denial and into recovery. This acceptance is what
the next stage is all about. Yet we still have one more small
action to take in gaining awareness. Before you end this
meeting with your partner, we want you to look at one
more area for undelivered communications.

What about the things you have discovered since the
loss? Many times widows find that they weren't well prepared for independent life following a death. They may be
angry at their spouses because of it. We often hear widows
talk about how their husbands told them everything was
taken care of financially; after the death, the widow finds
out this isn't true. Sometimes widows and widowers feel
as if they gave up some of their own personality and
creativity in order to stay married. They don't feel this
way until after the death; then they become upset. For full
recovery to be achieved, it is imperative that these things
be communicated to your partner.

One lady we know found out that her husband had

had an affair. She didn't learn about it until three weeks after his death. She kept the feelings of anger and betrayal inside. Within months of his death she developed a severe arthritic condition. As she began to take a closer look, she realized something had been wrong in her marriage, but she had never wanted to confront the issue. She never wanted to accept responsibility for participating in her anger. She was afraid. Her fear and isolation kept her from realizing that other possible choices remained available to her.

When Frank's sister died, many of her old friends showed up for the funeral. One of these friends reminded Frank of the time he got drunk at a party his sister gave in New York. In his drunken state Frank had completely blocked this memory out and still couldn't recall what had happened. Hearing the friend's story, Frank felt embarrassed about what he had done. This gave him one more unresolved issue in his relationship with his sister. Issues you have discovered since the loss should go on the third list of significant emotional statements undelivered.

At this point you have moved through the first stage of the recovery program. You have also begun a vital discovery in the second stage: you have gained absolute awareness that an incomplete relationship exists with a significant emotional loss in your life. It's one thing to understand what an incomplete relationship is and quite another to gain awareness of having one. It's the difference between reading a book about bike riding and having your first experience of riding one. You are not only aware that an incomplete emotional relationship exists, you have identified and communicated what you did and did not do to make it incomplete.

Now that you have this awareness, and now that another human being knows the truth, you can aquire a new perspective on the whole situation. It could take a while for this perspective to sink in, but once we have this awareness, it will never leave us.

Once you learn the system of how to recover, then you can apply it to every unresolved grieving experience that exists in your life. We know this sounds like a lot of work, and it is. The results will be worth it. Every grief experience not dealt with has a cumulative opposing effect on your aliveness and spontaneity. It's this accumulation of grief that has kept life from being the happy and joyous experience you want it to be. Only by identifying and resolving these issues will you be able to change the list of beliefs you discovered while sharing your Loss History Graph. Only by resolving these issues will you be able to have a life filled with meaning and purpose. Don't look at all these unresolved issues as if they were insurmountable. Look at them as an opportunity to remove barriers to your happiness and joy.

Actually, it's not such an overwhelming chore. When we look at a problem in its entirety, it often seems too large. Like trying to eat an elephant. How does one eat an elephant? There's only one way—one bite at a time. That's exactly the way you'll approach the unresolved losses in your life. One at a time, one step at a time.

9

Accepting Responsibility

Your lists of undelivered communications show the awareness you've gained about what is incomplete in your emotional relationship with the loss. The next stage is about accepting your share of responsibility for this incompleteness.

Frank was living in New York City when his father died in Texas. Frank's relationship with his father had been full of resentment and unresolved issues. The last happy event was a business trip his father took to New York City a few months before his death. Before that all encounters for the past two years between Frank and his father had culminated in upset. This trip ended devoid of any fighting, yet neither Frank nor his father could acknowledge this at the time. They felt good about not fighting but they could not address these feelings with one another. They were still in pain over not being able to communicate, yet it was not a conscious choice. It was all they knew how to do at the time. They had never been able to discuss their feelings with one another without fighting. Past experience had led them to believe that fighting was inevitable. As a result of their beliefs, they had no choice at all.

Accepting responsibility for not having told his father he was sorry for all the bad feelings was difficult for Frank and took some time. Frank had made his pride more important than feeling complete and resolved with his dad. In other words, he had made his position about what he felt to be right more important than his relationship with his father. After his father died, Frank wanted to choose again. Yet, how could he? When he talked to other people about the situation, the best advice he got was, "Well, that's just the way your father was. Don't blame yourself for what he couldn't give you."

Frank accepted this prescription as the only solution. He continued to make his pride more important than his need for emotional completion with his father. He failed to accept responsibility for this choice. As a result of his beliefs, he was unable to fully communicate his feelings and complete his relationship with his father.

What stands in the way of accepting this responsibility? We seem to ignore the most important assets we have—our relationships with those we love. We inventory everything in our lives. We inventory our wallets, refrigerators, record and tape collections; occasionally we service our automobiles and check the tires; sometimes we even balance our checkbooks. Your Loss History and Relationship graphs were inventories of your grief. These inventories led to a list of erroneous beliefs about loss and three lists of undelivered communications.

Where else have we been asked to really examine our lives and our relationships? How often do we stop and deliver communications that may seem trivial yet mean so much? When loss occurs, we could spend the rest of our lives berating ourselves and our loved ones for lacking the skill to communicate feelings.

This is absolutely the most difficult stage to move through. Accepting that we are responsible for our participation in any relationship during our adult lives is difficult. This statement is obviously true and easy to say, yet no human being we ever met could maintain this absolute acceptance 100 percent of the time. This ultimate goal is what growing relationships are all about.

To love someone unconditionally is the virtuous thing to work for in any relationship. But to stand up for what you believe to be moral and right is also important. What do we do when the two collide? Something has to give or someone is going to suffer. Many times both parties in a relationship suffer. They may not consciously suffer, they may not be aware of their feelings, they may actually seem to be numb. Yet the pain is there, and pain never feels good, happy, joyous, or free. The pain is there as a result of their beliefs.

If the parties don't suffer, it's because they are completely aware of and take full responsibility for the position they've chosen. Either they consciously choose to make their love for the relationship more important than what they believe to be right, or they consciously choose to make their beliefs more important than the relationship. It is simply a choice. It's not right or wrong; it's a choice they usually base on what they perceive is going to make them feel the best. Maturity in relationships is knowing which choice will feel best the longest. This conscious awareness of our beliefs and acceptance of our responsibility in relationships is so difficult and yet so vital in our recovery process.

Our experience has been that when people willingly commit themselves to life, recovery, and peace of mind, the right choice for them will be revealed. The right choice for them will allow the most amount of recovery and freedom for the longest period of time. Letting go of our position and accepting responsibility for what we have or have not done in completing our relationships allows us the freedom to discover the full potential of ourselves and others. This knowledge requires much willingness and faith— faith that freedom, happiness, and joy are our birthrights.

One of the positive events in John's relationship with his father was a small surprise party that his dad gave for him:

"I played high school basketball and we had just won a holiday tournament. When I arrived home, my father had invited some of my friends over. They surprised me with a party. For whatever reason, this party was important to me. That my father would go to all that work was important to me. While doing the Relationship Graph, I realized that I'd never told him how much I appreciated his thoughtfulness. I tried to tell him, but comments about feelings made him nervous so he found a reason to walk away.

"I should've pursued it. It was one of the things which I wished I had done. I was going to, but something came up and I put it off. Then our relationship changed, my parents were divorced, and somehow I never told him about my feelings. When he died, it came to me that I wished it had been handled differently."

To this day John doesn't know why the party his dad gave for him was so important. He didn't need to know why. Indeed, trying to figure out why is a waste of time. He did know it was important and he knew that the beliefs he had about communicating his feelings led to this undelivered communication.

STEP ELEVEN: IDENTIFYING UNDELIVERED COMMUNICATIONS

We're now asking you to look at the three lists you made after sharing your Relationship Graph: the list of positive things that were not acknowledged; the list of negative things that were not spoken about; and the list of all the things you wish you could have said but didn't.

In all three categories ask yourself these questions:

• Which of these undelivered communications have you thought about before?

• Which of them did you consider discussing with your loved ones before they died?

• Which ones did you put off because the time wasn't right?

• Which ones did you start out to clean up but didn't because of the beliefs you had about what was the right thing to do?

Since making these lists and reading this chapter, have you thought of any new undelivered communications? We suggest you add them to your lists.

Whether there are many items on your lists or very few, all that matters is that you've tried to identify everything that wasn't acknowledged, verbalized, cleaned up, or settled. All that matters is that you begin to be willing to accept responsibility for your participation in creating the unfinished business on your lists. All that matters is that you become willing to accept that there were many opportunities to express your thoughts and feelings.

Remember the list of erroneous beliefs you made when sharing your Loss History Graph? If you'll look at those beliefs and then look at the unresolved issues on your three lists, you will see why it is impossible for you to remain complete in relationships. These beliefs keep you from communicating honestly, if at all, especially with those who are closest to you. As a reminder, here's John's list:

1. Bury your feelings
2. Replace the loss
3. Grieve alone
4. Just give it time
5. Regret the past (DIFFERENT, BETTER, OR MORE)
6. Don't trust

Honestly ask yourself how it would be possible to think that people adhering to any one of these six beliefs could become emotionally complete in their relationships. In fact, due to our socialization and beliefs, most of us carry around undelivered communications for many of the important people in our current lives. Once we accept responsibility, we can make new choices in these relationships.

Right now, the most important thing is for you to recognize your part in not discussing issues or expressing feelings. This is an examination of yourself, not an examination of the deceased. However, doing this work on an incomplete emotional relationship with a loss doesn't mean that you should now be beating up on yourself or being self-critical. There is no benefit in doing either. If you are scolding yourself, stop it and get support from your partner! You'll have more forgiveness for your partner's part in creating the items on his or her list than you'll have for your part in creating the unresolved issues on your list. If your partner feels bad in response to reading this part of the handbook or feels bad about the things he or she has listed, your first response will probably be: "Gosh, that's okay, you just did the best you could."

So why not feel this way about yourself? When you get to the bottom of it all, you'll know you honestly did the best you could with what you had at the time. The same is true for loved ones that die. They did the best they could, too. Perhaps you feel this wasn't good enough—are you willing to accept that it's true?

STEP TWELVE: SHARING UNDELIVERED COMMUNICATIONS

Once you've made your lists, you need to do some work with what you've discovered. Have another meeting with your partner. Discuss what you've read in this chapter. Evaluate your lists again. Evaluate each other's willingness to accept responsibility in these unresolved issues. In this case acceptance means looking honestly at the truth. Look at your list of beliefs and look at your undelivered communications. Discuss what being willing to accept responsibility for the choices you've made means to you.

WILLINGNESS

The willingness to accept responsibility for your participation in not delivering these communications is imperative in this step of your recovery. We are asking for the willingness to accept responsibility. Absolute acceptance at this point is not necessary, but willingness is. Without this willingness, it is impossible for you to move beyond this stage of your recovery.

Your ability to be honest with your partner about accepting responsibility for your feelings and actions must continue to improve or recovery is impossible. Accepting responsibility for your participation in an incomplete relationship means discovering the willingness within yourself to acknowledge your role in not having communicated these things to your loved one. *Let it go.*

Finding the willingness within was the theme of a personal composition Frank wrote for our quarterly newsletter. You, too, might want to try writing about your understanding of willingness and acceptance.

AN INSIDE JOB

As a direct result of all I've lost and all I've accepted I've become a new person. My reactions are different. I'm more aware. I like this new person much better than the old one. Prior to my recovery, I never thought I would feel this way.

Losses have caused the greatest changes in my life. The greater the loss the greater the change. Changes scare me. The more adjusted I become to things outside being a certain way, the harder it is to let them change. I have consistently needed a better understanding of myself to accept changes.

I can recall needing a better understanding of myself when I was twelve years old. My family had taken an overseas trip for the summer. A combination of my adolescence and a drastic change of environment felt scary to me, not unlike the feelings of grief I was to have when my sister, father, uncle, grandparents, or friends in Vietnam died. But the grief from death was much more severe because of the tremendous shock involved. The changes I was experiencing at twelve were much slower in coming and therefore the grief was less intense, yet just as real. I had to stop and reevaluate things. How could I accept this? How was I going to relate to the rest of the world? Who was I to the world around me? How did I fit into the scheme of things?

Looking back, I realize this was the beginning of a spiritual experience. Up to the writing of this article, and hopefully beyond, this experience continues to change and grow within me. For thousands of years spiritual texts have told us the kingdom of heaven is within each of us, and that only through loving others is it revealed. The changes that occur are an inside job resulting from my acceptance of the outside.

My search for acceptance has been and continues to be quite a journey. This journey reminds me for one more day that my happiness is an inside job. My happiness depends on the choice within me to not fight with changes beyond my control. My happiness depends on my willingness to accept these changes. To be happy is all I ever wanted. The secret is to keep it the priority. The secret is to remember that happiness only comes when I accept that which just seems impossible to accept. I don't need to accept it for the rest of my life, just for today.

It's so simple. Like having a rose garden. It is impossible to have a rose garden and not experience pain and joy in working with it. It is impossible to maintain a rose garden and not get results. The garden can be neglected for years and yet the roses will still try to grow. It takes more than time to clean up a rose garden. It takes willingness and acceptance to do the work. With these things it takes much less time than I originally thought. To feel better in such a short amount of time is grace. It seems like so much work until I get started. Only then do the results become a reality.

This story characterizes my personal experience of willingness and acceptance better than anything else I could offer. It's about three little fish in a very large ocean. These three fish lived where the water was warm. They were swimming around the harbor one beautiful morning. Their bellies were full, the weather was great, they had each other, and nothing was lacking in their lives. Yet, they felt incomplete.

They felt there was something missing. About that time a large, old, and wise fish swam by. He looked at these three and said, "Good morning all, isn't the water fine this morning."

Our three friends looked at one another and watched this big fish swim off. A few moments later, one of them said, "Did you hear that guy? He said something about water. What's water?"

"I don't know. I never heard of it."

The third fish said, "Neither have I."

These three fish proceeded to swim all over this very large ocean looking for water. It was inside of them and outside of them all at the same time. They were looking through water for water.

Finally, after much searching, one of the three became tired and discouraged. The other two stopped to help. In one magic moment between the three of them, they saw the water. They found what they were looking for. It had been there all along. Only when they stopped searching were they able to see it. Only in forgetting themselves and being of service to one another was it revealed. Only through a daily commitment to maintain their awareness of this discovery could they feel complete, happy, joyous, and free.

The longer I go without honestly accepting the changes around me, the more I lose touch with the fact that happiness is an inside job. Not accepting changes beyond my control is painful. Sometimes I feel like a glutton for punishment. It's as though I refuse to explore beyond the mundane thoughts in my head to a place much deeper inside of me. The more I go inside, the more I find a source that I never knew was there. I consistently experience a simplicity about life when I start and end my day feeling this source. Through this source I know my grief is going to pass. Through this source I find I can give something today, just for today, just for the simple act of giving. Whenever I go inside and find something to give, as small as it may seem at first, I know I need nothing on the outside to fix me. May I never lose my ability to reach inside and find that place of continued inspiration.

10

Identifying Recovery Communications

One of the most amazing things we've watched over the years is the actions people take just before they die. They're consumed with the need to clean it all up before time runs out. We've seen people hang on for several hours while a close friend or relative comes from some great distance, so they can do the work that must be done. The things that need to be settled are usually never big things; they seldom take long to communicate. It's as if the severity of the moment wipes out all the old ideas about not communicating or showing feelings.

After the dying person has said what needs to be said, he or she will almost always find a way to die alone. So many times we've heard grievers say:

> *"I was with him every moment, and the one time I left the room, he died."*

> *"I was with him for forty-eight hours straight. I went home to change clothes, and as soon as I got home, the hospital called to say he had died."*

> *"The one time I left the room for coffee, he died."*

"I let my sister go in to see her. I thought there'd be time later."

Dying alone is what happens for most patients. It is possible that the dying person is emotionally complete and feels that dying alone will make it easier for the loved one.

This desire on the part of the dying person to clean things up was talked about at the 1984 Democratic National Convention. The Reverend Jesse Jackson told the convention about going to visit Hubert Humphrey before his death. When he went in to see Vice President Humphrey, he found him talking on the phone. He was cleaning up any and all misunderstandings before it was too late. Reverend Jackson went on to say that Humphrey had a clipboard with names on it, and he was checking them off as he spoke with each person.

There are only three areas in which we can be emotionally incomplete:

1. Making Amends—things that we're sorry for either having said or done, or not having said or done.

2. Offering Forgiveness—things we need to forgive others for, either real or imagined.

3. Expressing Significant Emotional Statements— that we need or want to say. ("I love you," "I thank you," "I was proud of you," etc.)

We call these three categories Amends, Forgiveness, and Significant Emotional Statements. Many times these categories correspond with the three lists you started in your Relationship Graph and completed in the last chapter:

1. Amends—above-the-line events (happy/positive).

2. Forgiveness—below-the-line events (unhappy/negative).

3. Significant Emotional Statements—other undelivered communications.

MAKING AMENDS

This is the only category that can shift from above-the-line events (happy/positive) or below-the-line events (unhappy/negative). We can be sorry for not having acknowledged a positive event. Yet, we can also be sorry for our part in creating a negative event. In either case this category will be a major portion of your undelivered communications.

Examining undelivered amends can lead to expanded awareness of when to change your behavior. This is because making amends is more than saying you're sorry. We can remember as kids, adults telling us to say we were sorry for something we'd done. To appease the adult, we would say we were sorry, wait for the adult to turn away, and then promptly do it again. This isn't making amends. This is saying you're sorry and not changing your behavior. Making amends is saying you're sorry *and* being willing to change your behavior. It's saying you're sorry and then backing it up with action.

This gives us an enhanced sense of freedom. It's like finding the resources to pay all of our debts. The resources come when we are willing to do all that we can to make our amends. When amends are made and our behavior has changed, there's no more looking back and no more need to protect ourselves. We need no more explanations. There are no more regrets. We know we've done all that we can do. This is the greatest gift we can give ourselves.

OFFERING FORGIVENESS

Now let's look at the Forgiveness category (unhappy/ negative). To do this, John will tell a story about the death of his father:

"For many reasons my relationship with my father wasn't in good shape when he died. My parents had been divorced and my dad had moved away. He had changed his lifestyle and I had judged him harshly for it. We had not spoken often or lovingly for several years. The day before he died, he asked a nurse in the hospital to call me and see if I would come and visit him.

"Because of my anger, it took me a couple of hours to decide to go. I eventually went, and when I saw him I was shocked at how he looked. I sat by the bed and waited for him to wake up. When he did, I leaned over him so he could see who was there. In a small, weak voice he said, "Son, if I had known any better, I would have done better."

While John was considering the implications of that statement, his father died.

"To the best of my father's ability he was trying to clean things up between us. I spent the next few

minutes deciding that in fact it was true that he
had always done the best he could with what he
had known. It wouldn't do me any good to wish
that he had known more. He was acknowledging
his amends; he was trying to say he wasn't perfect.
It was a brave thing for him to do.

"Before they came to take his body away, I
cleaned up my unfinished emotional business with
him. I can't tell you how grateful I am that I got
that chance. I learned many precious lessons in
those few minutes which would be of great value to
me later."

John didn't forgive his father for his father's sake; he for-
gave him for himself. If he hadn't, he'd still be dragging
his anger around with him. That anger would still be re-
stricting his life. He'd be the loser.

How can there be meaning, purpose, happiness, and
joy if anger and resentment stand in the way? This is a
difficult hurdle to cross because we're so very practiced at
making others responsible for our feelings. The problem
stems from our deeply rooted need to be right. Remember, at some point each of us must accept our share of
responsibility.

In order to be successful in our recovery, we must be
clear on several things where forgiveness is concerned:

- You have some erroneous beliefs—so has everyone
  else.

- You've made mistakes—so has everyone else.

- In order to forgive yourself, you must forgive
  others.

The transgressions which you must forgive fall into one of two areas: they are either *real* or they are *imagined*. Considering the mistaken ideas we have about how other people are responsible for the way we feel, there is a fair chance that much of what we need to forgive is imagined.

Here's an example we use in our seminars to explain nonverbal communication. It's also a great example of imagined transgressions. Both of us are married. Sometimes after coming home from work, we'll know that our wives have not had a very good day—they will tell us so without saying a word. Something about the way a pot is being placed on the stove or something about the way a door is being shut clearly communicates that this day has not been a happy, joyous, and free experience for them.

Before learning the hard way, we used to react by saying, "What's wrong?"

And their standard response was, "Nothing."

A lot of communication here. At dinner the conversation would go something like this:

"Pass the salad."

"Get it yourself."

We'd go to bed that night and though we were inches from one another, we felt miles apart.

Imagined transgressions are usually fairly clear once we get the right information. When we see that we gave another person the right to hurt us, we see that partial responsibility rests with us. When we realize that we haven't done a very good job of communicating our feelings, then we understand that the other party is not totally at fault. In order to forgive ourselves, we must first forgive others.

Therefore, the conversation could start something like this: "You know, sweetheart, when I come home and you're acting like this, it makes me wonder what I've done wrong. I've thought about it and if I've forgotten something, I'm sorry. I still don't remember what it was."

Now, no matter what the response is, there is a better chance of further conversation if we've begun with this statement. The statement acknowledges our partial responsibility for the situation and clearly communicates our feelings. This keeps our happiness from being the other person's responsibility. Nothing has been done to us, and the other person's upset is an imagined transgression.

Real transgressions usually occur prior to our adult lives and usually fall into the realm of physical violence or emotional deprivation. Real transgressions may be associated with some other problem caused by mental or emotional illness on the part of the transgressor.

For many, the real problem is the mistaken idea that to forgive is to condone. *Forgiving people does not mean endorsing their actions.*

If you grew up in an abusive home, the abuser was emotionally ill. If you grew up in an alcoholic home, the alcoholic had a disease. If you were molested, the molester was ill. Forgive the ill part of the person. We've talked to many people who were in therapy for years and had little success. Yet once they were able to separate the illness from the person, they began to make headway.

Nowhere do we say, nor should we say, that such behavior is condoned. You've already suffered enough from these situations; it's now time to forgive the illnesses and let them go.

SIGNIFICANT EMOTIONAL STATEMENTS

Finally, let's look at the Significant Emotional Statement category. This is the category in which there is almost always some level of emotional incompleteness. That's not surprising when you consider our poor ability to communicate feelings. We've already discussed how we try to make others responsible for our feelings. It's also true that most of our communication skills involve trying to get others to understand our point of view. What this has led to is an inability on our part to listen to what the other person is saying. We often listen to the first half of someone's communication and then prepare what we're going to say, instead of first hearing the second half. Another major problem is that we love so much but don't know how to say so. We've learned to talk in emotional shorthand.

The conversation goes like this. Mom or Dad says, "Why can't you get better grades?"

The child feels attacked and responds with sullenness or defiance. The truthful sentence could be, "We really love you and are afraid that if you don't get good grades, your life won't be successful."

That sentence is more truthful, expresses feelings, and doesn't sound like an attack. It allows room for further conversation. We can't tell you how many times we've heard a wife ask, "Do you love me?" And the husband responds, "Didn't I buy you that new coat?"

She asks about apples and he talks about eggs. A couple will come to see us, usually following the death of a child. We'll ask what we can do for them. The wife says, "We're developing a communication problem."

We'll glance at the husband and he says, "No, we aren't."

By his response he proves absolutely that a communication problem exists. Because of this emotional shorthand many people like to believe that their loved ones know how they feel about them. *Unless you tell people in plain English how you feel about them, they do not know.* For these reasons we're almost always caught with unfinished significant emotional statements—things we wish we had handled in ways that were DIFFERENT, BETTER, OR MORE.

STEP THIRTEEN: PREPARING YOUR RECOVERY COMMUNICATIONS

Now you're going to make one more set of lists. Get a clean sheet of paper. No one need ever see it. What you write is between you, this book, your sheet of paper, and the pen or pencil you're writing it with. On this sheet of paper you will compile the following items:

1. *Amends.* How many positive or negative events did you not make amends for? How many things did you find

that were happy events that you didn't acknowledge or thank your loved one for? Making amends for not having said "thank you" means putting a new emphasis on saying "thank you" today. Did you find negative events that you were responsible for? Making amends for these events means a willingness to change our behavior. It begins by accepting responsibility and delivering the communication. If you could have your loved ones back for one last conversation, would these things be important for you to say?

With each item on the amends list, what would it sound like if you had the chance to make your amends? Begin to write it out. Keep it simple. Here's an example:

> "Remember all the times I was late for our appointments? Well, I'm sorry. I'm doing all that I can to be more punctual. I know that being on time will give me a whole new sense of freedom. This is all I can do to make my amends."

How much better it feels to know you're on time and not in need of any more excuses for being late.

2. *Forgiveness.* How many things did you find on your negative/unhappy list? How many were not acknowledged or settled? If you had a chance, could you forgive? We are not interested in right or wrong. We are committed to your recovery. Do you want to be right or do you want to be happy?

Continue with your list and offer forgiveness. What would it sound like if these things were acknowledged? Write it out. Once again, keep it simple. Real transgressions could sound like this:

"I forgive you for the time you lied."

"I forgive you for the money you stole."

"I forgive you for all the times you hurt me."

Imagined transgressions sound more like amends:

"I'm sorry you were upset."

"I understand why you were running late and I'm sorry I got upset."

"I'm sorry I didn't trust you."

3. *Significant Emotional Statements.* How many significant emotional statements did you find? Aren't these the things you wish could have been said? If you could have your loved one back for one final conversation, would you want to say these things? What would it sound like?

Once again, look at your list. Make a note of any and all emotional statements that you wish you had said but didn't, or things you feel you were cheated out of on your last opportunity to communicate. These are your significant emotional statements. These are the things that are not complete.

Here's an example:

"I was so proud of your work."

"I loved you more than I could ever say."

"I never told you how important all the little things were."

"Thanks for all the cards you sent and presents you gave."

"Thanks for all the help in school."

STEP FOURTEEN: SHARING YOUR RECOVERY COMMUNICATIONS

Now that these three lists are done, it is a good time for you and your partner to have another meeting. Discuss what you have found. Help each other not to get caught in the need to be right. Forgiveness will be the area where you will need the greatest support from your partner. If nothing else, help each other to be willing to forgive the loved one's ignorance or illness. Once again, willingness is your beginning. You must remember that you have the courage, or you would not have come this far.

11

Taking Action

So far we have,

1. Gained Awareness that an incomplete emotional relationship exists.

2. Accepted Responsibility that in part we are the cause.

3. Identified Recovery Communications that have not been delivered.

The next step of our recovery will involve Taking Actions to deliver the recovery communications we have defined.

STEP FIFTEEN: WRITING A LETTER

Many of the grievers we have worked with have been given the suggestion of writing a farewell letter to their loved one. The ones who have tried it have often gotten some small amount of relief. Yet they found that in a short while the pain was back. Writing a letter, in and of itself, will not help. The important part is what's in the letter

148

and what your intent is. What should be included in a letter? Sergeant Friday used to say, "The facts, nothing but the facts."

We need to change that to "The truth, nothing but the truth."

The truth can only be discovered as the result of rigorous self-examination. Most of us, unfortunately, have little experience at this kind of self-scrutiny. As you move through this task, be as honest as you can be. Try to keep focused on the truth.

In case you are confused about what the proper intent is, it is to complete your emotional relationship with a loved one who has died. There is no need for you to debate whether you have this intent. If you've come this far in the steps, you have the intent.

We've talked with people who have tried writing a letter without moving through the first three stages of this program. What happens is that the letter results in all or nothing. Either the deceased was all good or all bad, or the griever is still making the deceased totally responsible for his or her feelings of emotional incompleteness. Recently we met a woman who wrote such a letter. She had been told by a friend that writing a letter would help her deal with the resentment she felt toward her dead father.

Our experience tells us this is a fairly common suggestion that comes from a loving place. The intent seems to be reassuring in seeking to complete an emotional relationship with someone who's died. To confirm the completion, the suggestion sometimes includes burning the letter. Although we do not see this symbolic gesture as necessary, its intention is correct: to complete the relationship. Yet this completion will not occur without our first taking responsibility for our part in the relationship.

Apparently this woman's father had exercised an inordinate amount of control over her life. And his last words before he died were, "I'll control your life even from the grave."

Some communication breakdowns are older than others. Theirs was long-standing and well practiced by both parties. The letter she wrote was a complete condemnation of her father; there was no forgiveness of any kind. Even though she was an adult and could have left home many times in the past, there was no acceptance of even minimal responsibility. So, right or wrong, the father did indeed continue to control his daughter from the grave.

Her letter-writing exercise was a futile effort that resulted in one more attempt at making someone else totally responsible for her feelings. It was one more unsuccessful try at recovery. In fact the letter was even more of a disaster than that. The suggestion to read and burn the letter became a symbolic gesture confirming her resentment, not completion. There was no gaining of awareness, no acceptance of responsibility, no offering of forgiveness. She put the letter in the fireplace, lit a match to it, and left the room. She felt better for about an hour. When she returned, guess what had not gone up in flames? The letter had only partially burned. The woman was convinced that her father was still controlling her life from the grave.

We don't want this letter to be an unsuccessful attempt at recovery for you. It's not a good idea to discuss what you're doing with anyone else except your partner. Friends and relatives may mean well, but they haven't read what you've read. They haven't done the work you've done. Please pay close attention to these instructions on what to say and how to proceed:

1. Writing the letter is best done alone, but we want you to let your partner know when you plan to do it. It is best done in one complete session. This is because writing the letter can be an emotionally painful experience and there is too much temptation to avoid the pain. Too much temptation not to forgive. Too much temptation not to move forward in your life. As long as you've come this far, please don't lose it now. You've already proven your courage; use it now to write this letter.

The pain you may feel must be confronted directly. It's okay to cry. It's okay to feel bad. Don't be surprised if you feel relief as you go along. It's not as if you haven't thought about these things before. Many people have known for a long time what wasn't emotionally complete; they just didn't know what to do about it.

2. Before beginning sit down, take three deep breaths, and relax. Pull out the list of communications you defined in Step 13. These statements include:

- Amends
- Forgiveness
- Significant Emotional Statements

Read what you've written. Refresh your memory about what's incomplete. When you're done reviewing these defined statements, place them aside, take three more deep breaths, and relax.

3. Write this letter as if your loved one were still alive and could hear the letter being read. What might he or she say in response? What would you say in response to that? We want you to be as thorough as you can. The key is to write about what is emotionally incomplete. You have now accepted responsibility for your part in this incompleteness. What would it sound like to communicate this to your loved one? Write to the person who really was, not to the person you wish had been.

4. You can write as much as you feel the need to write. You're going to have your loved one back for one last conversation, so let's make sure we get everything said that needs to be said. If you get stuck, consult your three lists. If you're still stuck, write whatever you're thinking at the moment. We only want you to do this letter-writing exercise once, so be as complete as you know how. If we're going to err, let's err on the side of writing too much rather than too little. There is no sense in giving this a half attempt. Go for broke.

5. You'll know that you're finished when you can write "I love you" and feel as if there is nothing more to say. If you can't, keep going. Eventually, you'll arrive at the end. Eventually, "I love you" will be all that's left to say. Now it's time to pick up your pen and begin.

STEP SIXTEEN: SAYING GOODBYE

As we said earlier, letter writing could have been suggested to you before. Our experience has shown us that this suggestion doesn't work for two reasons:

First, the intent of the letter must be to complete an emotional relationship by acknowledging

- Awareness of what an incomplete relationship is.
- Acceptance of responsibility for your role in its incompletion.
- Recovery communications that have not been delivered.

And second, since another human being never hears the letter, it's not communicated.

Does a tree falling in the forest make noise when no one is there to hear it? In order for something to be communicated, it must be heard. In order for an emotional relationship to be complete, it must be communicated. The impact of the spoken word on the mind of the listener is absolutely necessary for recovery to be achieved. If another living human being never heard the letter you wrote, it was never communicated. You cannot recover alone. Reading a letter alone to a memento, picture, grave, or memory is nothing more than a daydream.

When was the last time you caught yourself daydreaming? When was the last time you had an intense conversation with someone by yourself? When was the last time you were alone and had an argument with someone while driving the car, making dinner, or taking a shower? When was the last time you worried about something in the future that you knew you couldn't do anything about? We all do these things as a normal part of our adult lives.

Any time your mind and body are not in the same place at the same time, it's a fantasy. We're all good at fantasy games—we just don't like to admit it. Remember when we were kids? We talked about our fantasies all the time. We shared them with others. Remember playing make-believe? We were cowboys, soldiers at war; our dolls were real, we talked to them, we had an imaginary friend when we were alone; we had one when we weren't alone. We were kids then. We want you and your partner to be kids again. We're going to play make-believe.

With the help of your partner, you're going to use a verbal fantasy game to complete your emotional relationship with your loved one. The idea is to back up the clock: in order to reach out for your loved one and find him or her there; in order to get it all said before it's too late; in order to clean up verbally all the things you wish were DIFFERENT, BETTER, OR MORE. Please take no shortcuts with this exercise. Set yourself up to succeed.

Here are the instructions:

1. Pick a location for the game. Where was your last conversation with your loved one? If you can't go there, what's the next best place? You'd be amazed what hospitals will let you do. If you don't remember the last conversation, what location reminds you of your loved one? Where would he or she like to have this letter read? It can be set in any number of places: a favorite room, a favorite spot outside that had meaning for you and your loved one. It could be at the

cemetery if that will help you feel close to your loved one. You can use pictures. It's a game—the sky's the limit. Let your partner know what the setting is going to be for this most important conversation.

2. Pick a time for the game that works for you and your partner. If the location is not the exact setting you want, when you get there tell your partner about it. What's missing? Let your partner support you in making believe the stage is set just as you want it.

3. Tell your partner about the last conversation you remember having with your loved one. To the best of your ability tell your partner what was said. Explain all the details. Make sure both of you understand the details. How did the conversation go? How did you want it to go? Try to see your loved one in your mind's eye. Tell your partner what your loved one looks like. Pretend that he or she is really there. Once the three of you are present, what do you want to say?

4. Read your letter. If in the back of your mind a little voice starts telling you this won't work, don't listen. If you listen, you lose. The real issue is trust. This is not new. Fantasy letters have been used for centuries, and this time you've done the necessary actions first. You don't get to know if you can feel better until after you take recovery action. Your willingness to recover is no longer in question—look how far you've come. Don't stop now. What do you really want to say? If your throat gets tight, keep going. Talk while you cry.

5. If you're the listener, don't interrupt. Don't hug, don't touch, don't hand your partner a tissue, don't

distract your partner in any way. The process of re-
lease of feelings will work best this way.

6. Let it be okay that you cry while you read.
Remember your commitment to complete your emotional relationship with your loved one. When you get
to the end of the letter and say, "I love you," then it's
time to say your final goodbye.

7. Look at your partner, see your loved one, tell
him or her goodbye. Not goodbye to the fond memories. Not goodbye to your spiritual beliefs. Goodbye to
the emotional incompleteness. Goodbye to the pain,
isolation, and confusion. Goodbye to the physical relationship that you had but that has now ended. Say
goodbye and then let it be okay that you cry and let
it all out.

8. You'll feel an enormous sense of relief. It will
feel like a 500-pound weight has been lifted from your
back. You'll get to know what a balloon feels like when
it lifts off. Don't be surprised if you smile and laugh in
a very short time. You've just let go of carrying a big
load. Give your partner a hug. Know that you have
made a powerful decision and taken action to recover.

We could write another book of success stories from
the accounts of grievers who have followed the steps pre-
sented in this handbook. Here are just two examples:

"My son died seven years before I found this
program. He was hit and killed by a truck while
riding home from his high school football practice.
My wife and I spoke very little after this time. On
my son's birthday and during holidays I would find

my wife or she would find me sitting on the bed in his room. It was next to our bedroom upstairs in the house. We had kept it locked and untouched. We gained weight, my wife lost interest in the house and community activities, I lost interest in my job.

"I am a health-care professional, and a colleague of mine told me about a seminar on how better to talk to grievers about death. I told him I would go to learn the counseling techniques, but I knew I was going to deal with the death of my son. Upon returning, I sent my wife to the seminar. She was reluctant at first, yet she could tell a definite difference in my attitude.

"We have now said goodbye to our son. It is impossible in this short space to tell you the difference it has made in our lives. My wife and I take a walk together every morning. I'm more in love with my work than ever before. My wife has resumed her volunteering. We currently sponsor three children in refugee camps. Our son's old bedroom is now a game room. We took the wall out between the rooms and installed a full-size billiard table. We are today the parents our son would have wanted us to be."

We'll narrate the second story, which is about a woman who called us recently. Her husband had died thirteen years ago and she hadn't felt right since. She took the steps laid out in this book and completed her unfinished relationship with her husband. Two months later, she attended a christening for her nephew. The boy was being named after her husband—this was not an event she was looking forward to.

To her surprise she called to tell us it wasn't the cause of a sad memory for her but instead was a wonderful experience. She was able to clear up some unfinished business with her in-laws. Some resentments had been separating them ever since the death.

How Far You've Come

We get to hear these success stories all the time at the Institute. They're what keep us going. You don't get to really understand how these stories can be true until after you've done the work. If you have done the work, this is how far you've come:

- You have gained awareness that an incomplete emotional relationship existed between you and a significant loss; awareness that society does not teach us how to deal with loss but rather how to acquire and hold on to things, and awareness that this leads to others, through their own ignorance, teaching us how to "ACT recovered."

- You have accepted responsibility for your part in maintaining an incomplete relationship with this loss. You have found the courage within yourself to communicate this responsibility to your partner.

- You have defined recovery communications undelivered to your loved one: things you wish had been DIFFERENT, BETTER, OR MORE; and happy times, not-so-happy times, and all the significant emotional statements that were so important to say.

- You have now taken actions to communicate these things by making your amends, offering forgiveness, and having one last conversation that allows you to say goodbye.

- And you are about to move beyond loss by reading the last chapter of this handbook with your partner and by sharing with others what you have found. Thank you.

12

Moving Beyond Loss

The last stage of the program is all about sustaining your new perspective. This consists of creating and maintaining an environment that reflects your completion of the loss. Soon people will see, if they haven't already, the effect your completion has on your aliveness and spontaneity. This chapter will give you suggestions on helping others to move beyond loss.

CLEAN-UP WORK

A new perspective leads to things looking different. They look different because we have changed on the inside. Completing our relationship brought about this change. Since the inside has changed, it will now be necessary to look at the outside. You'll want to adjust your environment to reflect this new inside perspective on the loss. Completing your relationship changes things from the inside out.

When Frank was twelve years old, his family took a three-month trip around the world. Until that time most of his activities had consisted of riding a bike, going to school, and playing with family and friends at home. His experience on the trip led to completing many old and limited ideas he had about the world. Upon returning, he immediately went back to school and found that his entire perspective had changed. His house looked smaller; the backyard had shrunk; his bike looked puny; the classrooms at his school didn't seem to fit any more. The trip had changed his perspective. Everything on the outside now looked different.

The first step in our clean-up work will be to look at outside reminders of the loss. Earlier we referred to grievers who hold on to objects which represent the deceased loved one. We called this "enshrinement." We hold on to these things when we're emotionally incomplete with the loss. There will now be no need to hold on to these objects with such intensity. Some of the objects won't seem to fit with your new perspective; these are the ones you'll want to get rid of. It is normal to want to keep some things and not be sure about others.

Perhaps helpful friends have told us to just get rid of it all—clothes, mementos, everything. But we don't want to get rid of it all. We may remember trying several times, but it was so painful we had to stop. We wanted everyone to think we were doing well, so we hid the fact that we hadn't gotten rid of these things.

One woman we met told us a story of how she made a mistake in disposing of her husband's effects. Everyone kept telling her she had to get rid of all his things. She wanted to do what was right. So, one day she drank four bottles of beer to get up the courage to do the job. In her half-drunken state, she threw away everything. She regretted this action the very next day, but by then it was too late.

Before you rush out to throw everything away, let's make a plan of how to accomplish this goal. The all-or-nothing approach isn't part of it. One widow had a picture of her husband hanging in the bedroom. Her husband died at three o'clock in the morning. At that exact time she'd wake up and the first thing she'd see was his picture; she found it impossible to get back to sleep. When she mentioned this to a friend, the friend said she should get rid of it. Now the woman couldn't bear to do that, but she didn't know what else to do. Fortunately, someone told her about the work we do. After hearing the problem, we suggested she simply move the picture to a different location in the house. She thought this was the best idea she'd ever heard. She wanted to know why she hadn't thought of the solution herself.

The answer is that she was grieving. She was so close to the problem that she couldn't see it. She was the one in emotional pain and it clouded her judgment.

It's this kind of small and simple approach that we want to use on all the things that need to be taken care of. Also keep in mind, never alone. Perhaps we'd better say that again so you get the point—NEVER ALONE! Now that you and your partner are in this together, help each other. Don't offer advice, just help with the work and listen when your friend wants to talk. Many of these chores will stir intense feelings—feelings that must not be suppressed.

DISPOSING OF CLOTHES—THE PILE PLAN One of the most painful tasks for grievers is deciding what to do with the clothes. One good approach has been called the ABC

Plan. This approach can also be used for other personal belongings. It has also been lovingly referred to as the Pile Plan. You'll see why as we go along.

Remember, the objective is to end up with what you want to keep without keeping things you don't need or want. So, take all the clothes and put them in the living room. Do we mean physically move all the clothes? Yes, that's exactly what we mean. With your partner, go through them one at a time. Make three piles of clothes. If you want to talk about a memory that one of the articles stimulates for you, please do so with your partner. The piles should be grouped as follows:

Pile A contains the things that you are certain you want to keep.

Pile B contains the things that you are certain you want to dispose of. Things to sell. Things to give to other family members. Things to give to charity or the church.

Pile C contains all those things that you're not sure about yet. If there is any doubt at all about which pile an item goes in, it goes in pile C.

We are not in a race. We're employing a clear plan that works. As you stand in the room looking at all the clothes, it may dawn on you why some people refer to this as the Pile plan. Dispose of the piles as follows:

Pile A goes back in the closet.

Pile B is given to individuals, groups, etc.

Pile C goes into bags and boxes and to the garage or the attic.

Then congratulate yourself and thank your partner. Next week, go to your partner's house and do the same with his or her things. One month later, bring all the pile C bags and boxes back into the living room and work the plan all over again. Once again, never alone! Pile A is for the few things you find that you want to keep. Pile B is for those things you are sure you want to discard. Everything else goes back into the bags and boxes, and back into the garage or attic. Doing this task one more time will accomplish your goal of keeping what you want to keep and not retaining things that you don't need.

THE NEW-ACCOUNT SOLUTION Another problem that people have trouble with is the checking account with their loved one's name on it. It's fine if you don't want to change the account name. Yet many spouses find that changing the name generates a desired feeling of independence. Once again, people often attack this problem from the wrong direction. Instead of taking your loved one's name off the checking account, open a new one. Each month, make sure some of your transactions are done through the new account. In no time at all you'll have a new pattern established and the old checks will no longer be a constant reminder of the loss. To open the new account go to the bank with your partner, never alone.

DEALING WITH ANNIVERSARY DATES Even after all the work you've done, there are still going to be certain occasions that will have the potential for making you sad. This is because you established a lot of familiar habits with your loved one. That's the bad news. The good news is that these times are usually predictable. We call them anniversary dates. They don't stand for conventional anniversaries. Any day that had significant meaning for you can be considered an anniversary date. Since we almost always know when they're coming, we can prepare for them.

The problem is in keeping your feelings to yourself. There is the temptation to try to handle these sad days alone. Don't do that. This comes from *thinking* you're recovered. You *are* recovered, and it's normal for recovered grievers to feel sad on anniversary dates.

Both you and your partner can start keeping a calendar for each other. Once a month, make a list of the upcoming dates that have potential for being sad. On those days make sure you are in contact. In grief recovery support groups this is done at each meeting. If you want to do it weekly, by all means do so. The birthday of the deceased, the date of death, the wedding anniversary, and holidays are all potential anniversary dates. For one woman we know, it was Thursdays—both she and her husband had jobs and Thursday was their day off together. It makes no difference what the day or occasion is. It only matters that you take a recovery action by calling your partner and not holding the feelings inside.

NEW PLACES, NEW TIMES   Another trap easy to fall into is that of familiar behavior patterns. In most relationships, social patterns develop. We go to see a movie at the same time every week. The same theater. If it's not the right movie, we rent a movie instead. We go home. We watch television—the same programs, with the same pizza or bowl of popcorn. We go to the same restaurant, see the same people, and eat the same food on the same day every week. Others know there's been a death, but they have no idea what to say. Therefore, they don't approach us in the same way or they don't approach us at all. To make it worse, we're alone. Same day, same time, same pattern.

Once again, do not use the all-or-nothing approach. Don't stop going to see movies. Don't stop going to restaurants. *Don't do it alone.* Try a different type of movie, something that you might like but never went to see because you knew your loved one didn't care for it. Try a different restaurant specializing in different foods. You might see some of the same people, yet the surroundings will be different. You'll feel different. You won't be alone and they won't be as uncomfortable approaching you. Introduce them to your partner or whomever you're with. If what you are doing hurts, stop doing it. Develop a new social pattern.

The solution is simple:

- Don't do it alone.
- If you think it might be painful, change it or don't do it at all.
- Check it out with your partner first.

FIVE QUICK STEPS

A woman we know in New York used to have lunch and then go shopping once a week with her daughter. Then her daughter died. Some time later, she met a young woman and was able to help this woman deal with the death of her husband. Now, once a week, they have lunch and go shopping.

After the two women had gone to lunch several times,

the young widow came to see the other woman. She was crying. She said she couldn't go to lunch any more: she had two small children and couldn't afford to spend the money. The older woman laughed. She had plenty of money and wanted to pay for the lunches, but she hadn't known how to ask her new friend without embarrassing her.

They both learned a valuable lesson about telling the truth. It has to do with disclosing the truth about your feelings and not being afraid. The young woman moved through the stages of this program with her problem:

1. She *gained awareness* that she was unhappy. She wanted to go to lunch with her friend, yet couldn't afford it any more. Her mind was telling her to come up with some other excuse. To stop showing up. Yet she didn't listen to it.

2. She *accepted responsibility* for her part in not being able to afford the lunches. She didn't isolate herself from the truth. She confronted the fear and embarrassment and swallowed her pride. She let it go. Her friend was going to have to understand or not be her friend any more. How was she going to tell her?

3. She *defined recovery communications* she could use to tell her friend. She role-played the conversation several times with another friend to make sure her communications were loving, and she simply told the truth. She didn't feel she owed amends, and she only herself to forgive.

4. She *took action* by going to her widowed friend and having the conversation. She let her feelings be

okay and simply told the truth. She discovered that the truth works.

5. She *moved beyond* this experience by calling her other friend and telling her what happened. She shared it again that week with yet another friend who was in pain—she shared the circumstances, the feelings, and the solution. She didn't give advice and she didn't tell her friend she knew how she felt. She simply told the truth about her experience and in doing so *gained more awareness.*

Another example of how the program works comes from Frank's mother. After her husband died, she discovered that it was *she* who had been leaving toothpaste on the bathroom mirror.

1. She immediately *gained awareness.* There was one more incompletion.

2. She *accepted responsibility* for her part in having complained about it.

3. This meant *defining recovery communications* by making amends, forgiving herself, and letting it go.

4. She *took action* by immediately calling her son and letting him know about her discovery. She said all the things she wished she could have said had her husband been alive.

5. She *moved beyond* this experience by sharing it with others. She *gained more awareness.*

This is how the program works. These are new labels for an old process. Grief and recovery have been around for centuries. Gain some awareness and you'll be in a position to gain more. The end is the beginning.

Support groups have found an easy way to remember these steps. They use the catchword AARAM (they pronounce it "ā´-ram"):

Awareness

Acceptance

Recovery

Action

Moving beyond

Helping Others Move Beyond Loss

Within two weeks following the death of a loved one, a griever has been pretty well isolated. People don't know what to say or do. So they do nothing.

Grievers begin to fall into the traps set by their storehouses of old beliefs. They feel alone, as if no one understands. You remember what that feels like. We've found that the sooner you can get a griever involved in recovery, the better. Keep your eyes and ears open. If you'll just talk about your recent recovery experience, you'll never run out of people to help.

You must go first. Don't ask others if they are ready to recover. It won't make any sense to them. They don't know if they'll even survive. You didn't think you'd survive the pain, but with the right information you did. Do what you know you need to do. Ask them to lunch. Call once a day and ask how they're doing. Don't judge, preach, or give advice. Just tell the truth about your own experience. Start putting their significant anniversary dates in your calendar. Call on those days. Share your feelings with them. Remember to share your feelings first, then ask how they're feeling. Don't ask them to go first; they've been evaluated and judged a lot. Tell the truth about your feelings and volunteer some of the smaller recovery actions you've taken.

Then give them the chance to give you their vote of confidence. Once they discover you're not going to criticize them, they'll introduce the topic of how they're feeling. If it looks as if they don't want to do their work with you, let it be okay. Grief recovery is a choice—and they may not be ready to choose yet.

If they are ready, become their partner or help them find another. If they find another partner and agree to do this work, ask them to call you on a regular basis. Find out how they're doing. Share your experience of recovery with them. Call them if they don't stay in touch. Ask them how it's going. Tell them that recovery does take some time, yet it need not take as much time as they have been led to believe. In short order you'll be able to see your own recovery as an event that enhances your ability to be of service to other drifting and solitary grievers—as an event that enhances your life and well-being. There is no greater thrill than to give hope and faith to those who have lost theirs.

STARTING A SUPPORT GROUP

It's not an impossible task; in fact, it's quite easy. We suggest you start small. You and your partner should each support one other griever. This will give you a support group of four. Meet once a week. Read this book a chapter at a time, taking turns with each paragraph. If any one of you finds another griever to join your group, it is not necessary to start the book over. Just pick up your reading from where you left off at the last meeting. This will give the new member a better overall sense of the program. Whatever you are reading that week will give him or her something to relate to or something to look forward to. Be sure he or she gets a partner and everyone's phone number, and make sure individual recovery starts from the beginning of the book. Do not adjust the entire group to the new griever. Spend an equal amount of time discussing where each partnership is with the recovery steps.

Start and end the meetings on time. We have found that one continuous sixty-minute segment or two forty-five-minute segments work best. As your group grows, you will want a moderator. We suggest that this responsibility rotate each week. Perhaps the moderator will host the meeting each week; in this way, the location and responsibility for refreshments will rotate, too. We've found that funeral homes, cemeteries, hospitals, and churches are more than willing to help grievers. You may be successful in approaching one of these institutions to help you share expenses and supply a location.

We have much experience in starting support groups and would love to hear from you. The Institute supplies a free quarterly newsletter to those on the mailing list. The articles and suggestions in this newsletter come from grievers and professionals like yourself.

Let us know how you're feeling. What changes have occurred in your life? Are you using your tools with your partner when a sad moment arrives? When you have a sad moment, are you accepting that in part you are the cause? Write to us, let us know what has happened for you. We'd love to be your friends. Our address is:

Grief Recovery Institute
8306 Wilshire Blvd. #21-A
Los Angeles, CA 90211

Most of the current programs at the Grief Recovery Institute are geared to the professional. We teach the professional a specific interview technique designed for grievers and their reaction to loss. If you are a professional reading this book, we would obviously love to hear from you, too.

We offer this handbook as a result of our personal recovery from loss. Our combined experience is the greatest gift we have to give. Your reading of this handbook has allowed us to give it. Thanks to your application of the steps in this handbook, we feel included in your recovery. Thank you for this gift to us. Grief recovery is no longer a neglected growth process in your life. May your recovery serve you as you continue along your path of personal growth. We are forever grateful for your participation.

Acknowledgments

Upon the completion of any book, there is cause for much gratitude. We wrote this book in partnership. Together, we want to acknowledge Barbara Bottner for her generous response in supporting the publishing of this work. We thank our literary agent, Christine Tomasino; our editor, Janet Goldstein; and the entire staff at Harper & Row for their commitment and dedication to the quality of this book. We also thank our friends in recovery—Tommy Atkinson, Dan Brintlinger, John Borgwardt, Duane Chambers, Steve and Terry Huston—for their courageous and loving support.

We would also like to express our individual thanks:

When we first started to write this book, I had no idea how much time and effort it would take. I'm afraid if I'd known, I probably would have given up. During the process of writing, I got a lot of support from a lot of people. There is no way I can mention all of them.

I want to thank Frank Cherry, my partner. I want to thank both my children, Allison (age 12) and Cole (age 6), for understanding, to the best of their ability, why I spent so much time in the den during the past six months. Allison understands fairly well what I do. Cole thinks I help sad people. In a way, I suppose he's right. I want to thank my former wife, Marcy, for going back into painful areas. Mostly, I want to thank my wife, Jess Walton. She has stood by me during this pioneering effort to help grievers. She's put up with my travel, long hours, and crying people in the living room. She's listened to me rant and rave when sentences would not flow. During all this, she's continued to work in her chosen field of acting. She is a glamorous person in a glamorous profession, and there's nothing glamorous about what I do. I know she understands but I want to thank her and tell her, *I love you,* anyway. Finally, I need and want to thank the thousands of grievers who've shared their pain, hopes, and dreams. Without their honest participation, there is no way this book could have been written.

John W. James

I wrote this acknowledgment during an editing session at 1:30 on a Saturday morning, Los Angeles time. We were under a deadline. My wife and children were home asleep. Since my work on this book began, I have been without them for many days and evenings. This has been my greatest sacrifice. If my writing this book has been an inconvenience or burden to my wife, Lisa, and daughter, Cecily, they have done a miraculous job

of not letting me know about it. My relationships
with Lisa and Cecily are two of the greatest gifts
I've ever received. To have them in my life is more
than I ever expected. I also want to thank my son,
Alexander. He was twenty-one months old at the
time of this writing. He has consistently expressed
his love by letting me know how much he misses
me. Someday he, too, will understand the necessity
of my taking this time from my family. I want to
acknowledge my mother, Kathryn. Her
contribution to my work is much greater than a
reading of this book will show. She continues to
inspire. I want to thank my partner, John W. James,
for being my best friend. Serving this Institute with
him has been, and continues to be, an honor and a
privilege. I want to acknowledge and thank
Milburn K. Bates for giving me the opportunity to
find my life's work. Most of all, I want to thank all
those who here must remain nameless—you know
who you are.

Frank Cherry